MAD, SA
MANA

For a complete list of Management Books 2000 titles,
visit our web-site on http://www.mb2000.com

Other Books by Adrian Furnham

Social situations (1981) (with Michael Argyle and Jean Graham)
The psychology of social situations (1981) (Edited with Michael Argyle)
Social behaviour in context (1986) (Edited)
The economic mind (1986) (with Alan Lewis)
Culture shock (1986) (with Stephen Bochner)
Personality Psychology in Europe (1986) (ed with Alois Angleitner and Guus van Heck)
Lay theories (1988)
The Protestant work ethic (1990)
Consumer profiles: an introduction to psychographics (1992) (with Barrie Gunter)
Personality at work (1992)
Biodata: biographical indicators of business performance (1993) (with Barrie Gunter and Russell Drakeley)
Reaching for the counter (1993)
Corporate assessment: auditing a company's personality (1993) (with Barne Gunter)
Business watching (1994) (with Barne Gunter)
Social psychology at work (1995) (edited with Peter Collett)
The new economic mind(1995) (with A. Lewis and P. Webley)
Why psychology? (1995) (with David Oakley)
Economic socialisation (1996) (edited with Peter Lunt)
The Myths of Management (1996)
All in the mind (1996)
Corporate culture shock (1997)
The psychology of behaviour at work (1997)
Children as consumers (1998) (with Barne Gunter)
The psychology of money (1998) (with Michael Argyle)
The psychology of managerial incompetence (1998)
Personality and social behaviour (1999) (with Patrick Heaven)
Body language at work (1999)
Designing and analysing questionnaires and surveys (2000) (with Chris Jackson)
The hopeless, hapless and helpless manager (2000)
The psychology of culture shock (2001) (with Stephen Bochner & V. Ward)
*Assessing potentia*l (2001) (with Barrie Gunter)
The 3D Manager: Dangerous, Derailed and Deranged (2000)

MAD, SAD AND BAD MANAGEMENT

A Lexicon of Corporate Cock-ups, Coincidences and Confusions

Adrian Furnham

2000

First published in 2003 by Management Books 2000 Ltd
Forge House, Limes Road
Kemble, Cirencester
Gloucestershire, GL7 6AD, UK
Tel: 0044 (0) 1285 771441/2
Fax: 0044 (0) 1285 771055
E-mail: m.b.2000@virgin.net
Web: mb2000.com

Printed and bound in Great Britain by Biddles, Guildford

British Library Cataloguing in Publication Data is available

ISBN 1-85252-415-4

Contents

Foreword

This book contains some fifty short essays of 800-2000 words on some aspect of modern business or management. It is prefaced by a satisfying aperitif and concluded with a substantial digestive. The theme is incompetence rather than competence; stupidity rather than wisdom; insanity rather than sanity. The sections examine some of the odd, bizarre and dangerous ideas, practices and beliefs of managers in all businesses.

They take, I hope, a disinterested and sceptical look at what managers and supervisors do at work. Someone observed that what he liked about Americans was their enthusiasm but what he did not like was their naivety. And, in turn, what he liked about the British was their scepticism but was less fond of their cynicism. The ideal was enthusiastic scepticism, not naive cynicism. The essays try to take an enthusiastic but sceptical look at management practice, managers and management science.

I believe scepticism and doubt are the first steps to knowledge. There is a fine journal called the *Sceptical Inquirer* which is subtitled 'Journal of the Committee for the Scientific Investigation of the Claims of the Paranormal'. Perhaps we need one called *The Sceptical Manager*: a journal dedicated to the Claims of Management Consultants and Gurus. Its task would be to apply reason, logic and scientific thinking to the claims of those who profess to know best about management and have silver bullet solutions to age-old, semi-intractable problems.

The source of inspiration for these essays is manifold. First there is the serious, if somewhat dull, academic literature on management. This is always most interesting when orthodox practices and beliefs are challenged and found to be wanting. Most business schools have lecturers on management who try to understand the complex business of business: defining, measuring, modelling ... to understand the consequences of various phenomena. Being a new 'science' (or at least social science), management writers are not as conservative, or paradigm-bound as colleagues in other disciplines. They tend not to follow the party line quite so slavishly partly because there is no real party line ... as yet. So more quirky, original (and often seriously wrong) articles get through the journal-editor police and make a stimulating and interesting read.

A second source of stimulation, far the more interesting and fecund, are popular, blockbuster, how-to-do-it, magic-solution books written by self-appointed experts. Some make their authors seriously rich. They are not marked by research, by carefully analysed case studies or by statistical analyses. Their evidence comes from those two most dubious of sources – anecdotes from others and personal experience. As we shall see, the plural of anecdote is not evidence. These books do not reflect doubt – in fact the very opposite. Their authors know the truth, which is surprisingly simple.

Paradoxically, in some senses they may be right. It is not difficult to list some dubious fundamental things managers have always and will always have to do to be at very least competent. They are not surprising counter-intentive or irrational – but that does not necessarily mean that people actually do them. Consider the following dozen. In the following list are simple, obvious pieces of management advice. They are straightforward, well known and do not require management consultant assistance.

1. Give employees the information they need to do the job.
2. Give all employees as much meaningful work as possible.
3. Pay people what they are worth in the market place.
4. Offer employees a share of the profits.
5. Demonstrate, where possible, long term employment commitment, development and promotion from within.
6. Provide regular specific feedback to staff on their performance.
7. Publicly recognise and personally congratulate employees after good work occurs.
8. Foster a sense of community and teamwork to ensure co-operation.
9. Be accessible to employees.
10. Ask employees for their feedback and ideas and involve them in the decision making as much as possible.
11. Pay attention to individual differences in terms of ability and personality and personal needs.
12. Use performance appraisals/behavioural measures as criteria to make decisions about promotion, PRP, training, etc.

A third source of inspiration for these essays comes from newspaper reports and magazine articles on managers and management. Typically, the articles tend to be eulogistic or damning. They praise and damn in equal measure.

But a good investigative journalist not only knows how to interview managers to really get them talking, but also they interview those who manage them and are managed by them. So one can get a really rich picture 'from the horse's mouth' on how both good and bad managers do their job.

Politicians, captains of industry, entrepreneurial 'wunder-kinds' and very rich business leaders are under close scrutiny for how they come to be that way. Some are remarkably inspirational; others very corrupt; some are seriously bright; others just very lucky. But some journalists 'get under the skin' of these people, really understanding their philosophy and foibles.

Lazy journalists are more likely to do advertorials for particular individuals or management concepts. No doubt primed by PR spin merchants and 'well treated' (read pretty nearly bribed) they uncritically accept what they are told, never challenging the meaning or interpretation.

The fourth source of evidence comes from consultants and consultancy. Many of my close friends gave up to academic life for that of consultancy. They tell interesting tales of what they do. Further, I get involved myself as part of my research endeavour into various topics like the validity of assessment centres, psychometric testing, training for creativity.

Often it can feel like being let into a dysfunctional marriage as a marriage counsellor. Asked to help with problems of absenteeism, or appraisal, turnover or theft, communication or corporate culture, one soon uncovers a long history of abuse, and incompetence. People who have not changed jobs tend to believe their work place is pretty average in the sense that what goes on is normal. They think what they experience is much the same for everybody, and they are often profoundly wrong.

It is a joke that consultants don't solve the problem they have been called in to cure but some other seemingly unrelated problem they do know something about and can (partly) solve. But it is true that often they are called in to solve problems that are symptoms of a much more serious malady. The patient is sometimes very ill indeed.

The diagnosis is often as difficult as the cure but really very interesting indeed. Consultants, like confessors (be they religious or marital), have privileged access to material that can give them an amazing insight into how organisational problems occur.

These essays have been scribbled in odd places – airport lounges, holiday resorts, seminar rooms. I have debated the issues most often with my very talented and intelligent wife ... herself a company director, consultant and psychologist. We have not always agreed on the cause, consequence or cure of the management incompetence, which is good; and very occasionally I have won the argument.

This book is for dipping into when the fancy takes. It aims to amuse, educate and infuriate. If you enjoy reading it half as much as I enjoyed writing, it I will be most satisfied.

Keep taking the tablets!

Adrian Furnham
London 2003

Aperitif

This collection of essays has one thing in common. It focuses particularly on people problems. Any inspection of a psychological library reveals that there are probably one hundred times as many books on depression as there are on happiness; on mal-adjustment rather than adjustment; on divorce rather than marriage; on the abnormal rather than the normal. Psychologists have argued that you best understand normality when it breaks down. Perhaps the same is true of management.

What goes on in the world of work is often astounding and bizarre. Alcoholics, psychopaths and depressives run businesses. The incidence of psychological problems among managers may be as high as, or even higher, than the incidence of these problems in the 'ordinary' population. And they can cause misery for millions.

It seems as if some sectors of industry either attract psychopathological incompetence or at least encourage it. For instance, obsessives are attracted to 'check-jobs' like quality control, health and safety and so on. Similarly technically expert introverts seem attracted to jobs that probably involve less people than computer interaction. Vocational guidance is fitting the job to the person and if the person is a 'little strange', there are some pretty odd jobs for them.

So one finds a clear homogeneity of types in certain, if not most, organisations – and for good reason. Sales organisations are full of extroverts; security organisations are full of those who border on the paranoid. But it is also possible that the organisation reinforces and rewards those behaviours. So the obsessives become more obsessional; the computer buffs exclusively email communications.

Thus one can find businesses that comprise like-minded people, comfortable in each other's presence and they way they do things. Some companies become paranoid and others depressive. And they may continue to be so until seriously pathologically disturbed and out of touch with reality. And this may be caused by just a few, difficult, demanding, deranged senior managers.

'Under New Management'

Most people have experienced the sudden, dramatic and disconcerting effects of a hotel, a restaurant or any other small service businesses 'changing hands'. In a matter of weeks, one can observe a massive change in process and product. Reliable, attentive service can easily turn into surly, resentful unhelpfulness (and of course, vice versa). The menu can change out of all recognition or worse, remain exactly the same except the food in quality, quantity and presentation is unrecognisable.

What is even more odd is that whilst the owners or managers may change, the staff remains the same. How is it that productive, satisfied staff can turn so quickly into an old style, In-Tourist-hotel from the Soviet days. (Recall – digestion is to indigestion as tourism is to In-Tourism).

The answer quite simply is management: style, values and behaviour. Indeed one of the signs one sees hanging outside restaurants, dry-cleaners and small shops is 'under new management'. They have usually been bought by people who believe that they can make a 'going concern' of any under-performing business by changing the management style.

Is it any different in big businesses? No, but the change takes longer. MBA students have various case studies showing the dramatic effect of a change of board. Sometimes it may be little more than the CEO but often he or she changes the people at the top, so in effect, you have a changed management team.

Because of their very bulk, it is said of oil tankers that their momentum requires that the skipper anticipates changes in direction as far as two to three miles before the ship responds. The same is true of very big organisations.

If a good manager puts in place procedures and processes that work, after a time one has a smooth operation; a happy ship; a nicely tuned engine. Replace the competent manager with one the precise opposite and it may take some time for the whole thing to fall apart. Bad managers commit sins of omission and commission. The former are probably more frequent: they let things slip: real staff meetings, appraisal, strategic planning, benchmarking. In these circumstances well trained staff simply carry on doing what they have been taught to do – but their efforts are ignored, unsupported or even punished. So they stop doing it.

More pernicious is the need of every manager to sweep with a new broom, to create an impression, usually to overturn all the policies, proceedings, processes and even products of the previous boss. This they believe justifies their appointment and demonstrates their uniqueness. Irrespective of the wisdom of the previous boss, the newcomer rattles the cage.

Of course they may be wise to do so. But they tend to do so indiscriminately.

A – Bad Management

There are at least two senses to the concept of bad management. It can be bad because of incompetence or it can be morally bad. The two are unrelated though they can co-occur. Both are frequent though the former is easier to see. Both are ubiquitous: they do not restrict themselves to any group, sector or time. The holy books of all religions detail the come-uppance of bad managers/leaders, though naturally they are usually concerned with moral transgressions.

One way to study how a process works is to study its opposite. Studying disease informs us about health; understanding the causes and consequences of depression tells us about happiness; maladjustment about adjustment. In this sense, stories about managerial ineptitude or moral lassitude tell us about their opposites. Management competence gives us a good insight into management incompetence; immoral and amoral managers, into those who uphold moral codes.

Management competence and incompetence

The word competent, like the word satisfactory, has a nice ‘ring’ to it – somewhat different from its dictionary definition. It has been taken over by inflationary superlatives so much so that to call somebody ‘competent’ at their job now sounds almost pejorative. It seems to imply average and mediocre, when everyone wants their staff and their service to be more than competent, i.e. excellent, outstanding and exemplary. Competence sounds like the 50th percentile and what one really wants is the 80th. Hence the fact that many companies have dropped in term.

With its allusion towards sufficiency and adequacy, the term ‘competence’ sounds dated in a world demanding excellence and outstanding performance. Some have argued that people can only infer competence from seeing incompetence. On the other hand, dictionary definitions do stress that competence is an ability, skill or know-how: something done in an efficient and effective or adequate way.

Whilst there may be difficulties in the technical definitions of competence, there are even more so when it comes to incompetence. Consider the following half dozen alternative meanings:

1. **Not having the competencies**: that is quite simply not having the abilities, traits or motivation to behave competently. Whether these are learnt or inherited is, of course, crucially important but the salient point for the definition is that the crucial, specified (core) competencies are missing.
2. **Not applying the competencies**: the definition suggests that a person has the necessary skills, abilities and traits that one might define as competence but chooses not to exercise them. This may be an individual or collective act. For instance 'work-to-rule' demonstrates a sort of volitional incompetence. On the other hand, it is possible, but unlikely, that people have latent competencies but do not 'apply' them through lack of awareness, but lack of self-confidence, or lack of opportunity.
3. **Having irrelevant or redundant competencies**: people may have been recruited and selected for a particular set of competencies that is now redundant. Jobs change as do the skills and attitudes required to do them. It is therefore possible that a person, once competent becomes less so to the point of incompetence.
4. **Being over-competent for the job**: most people have experienced being 'over-qualified' in every sense for the job. Some jobs that appear dull, routine, tedious or repetitive can wear can down the talented, skilled individual who performs them badly. The tasks do not stimulate or challenge the individuals who perform them at substandard rates.
5. **Being deliberately incompetent**: there are reasons why individuals or groups choose to behave in ways that are less than competent. They are often stimulated by feelings of anger, vengeance or inadequacy resulting from some perceived inequality at work. They may be doing so to reveal the importance of the role (when competently executed) to customers, colleagues or superiors.
6. **Not practising the competencies**: given that competencies are related to abilities and skills, they do require practice. If not exercised, they can, relatively easily and frequently, become rusty and hence a competency becomes an 'incompetency' - a lapsed skill.

There are sins of omission and commission with regard to being a bad manager. Bad, incompetent managers can be like that for many reasons.

B – Mad Management

Organisations that are set up to help victims of a particular mental illness and their relatives often try in addition to educate the public about the particular disorder, be they the psychoses, e.g. schizophrenia or manic depressive illness, the neuroses, e.g. phobia and depression, or the addictions, e.g. alcohol or narcotic dependence. They often produce (albeit somewhat dubious) figures about incidence in the population. And the shock is always the same: far more people have the problem that most people think. In this way they hope to make the abnormal look more normal.

Many people remark that, when reading psychiatric manuals or diagnostic criteria, they often feel they recognise themselves or others. They may be right. Consider the following, which are taken from a very well respected psychiatric manual. (DSM-IV-TR: published by the American Psychiatric Association). They consider the Personality Disorders. Personality disorders are not due to physiology and trauma, though they are often immune to treatment. It should be noted that the diagnostic criteria applied to these 'disorders' are very strict – psychiatrists need clear, objective evidence that nearly all the behaviours specified under each type are there. There are 10 in all. Read each and tick off the 6 or 7 signs of the disorder difficult to treat.

1. Paranoid Personality Disorder

Distrust and suspiciousness of others at work. The motives of all sorts of colleagues and bosses are interpreted as malevolent, all the time. The 'enemy' is both without and within.

(1) They suspect without much evidence that others are exploiting, harming or deceiving them about almost everything, both at work and at home.

(2) They are preoccupied with unjustified doubts about the loyalty or trustworthiness of subordinates, customers, bosses, shareholders and so on, on both big and small matters.

(3) They are reluctant to confide in others (peers at work) because of the fear that the information will be used against them, kept on file or used to sack them. They may even be wary of using email.

(4) They read hidden or threatening meanings into most benign remarks or events from emails to coffee-room gossip, and they remember them.

They are certainly hypersensitive to criticism.
(5) They persistently bear grudges against all sorts of people going back many years and can remember even the smallest slight.
(6) They perceive attacks on their character or reputation that others don't see and are quick to react angrily or to counter-attack. They seem hyper-alert and sensitive.
(7) They have recurrent suspicions, without justification, regarding fidelity of their sexual or business partners and can be pretty obsessed with sex.

2. Schizoid Personality Disorder

Here, managers seem detached from social relationships. They often have a restricted range of expression of emotions in interpersonal settings. They seem more emotionally flat rather than necessarily. They are thought of as 'cold fish', unresponsive, and desparately low in EQ.

(1) They neither desire nor enjoy close relationships at work, including being part of a family. They are never team players and hate the idea of being so.
(2) They almost always choose solitary activities, feeling uncomfortable even in informal gathering.
(3) They have little, if any, interest in having sexual contact with others – perhaps not a bad thing at work.
(4) They take pleasure in few, if any, activities. They seem joyless, passionless, emotionless.
(5) They lack close friends or confidants other than first-degree relatives. They are isolates at work but apparently not unhappy with their friendlessness.
(6) They appear indifferent to the praise or criticism of others. Absolutely nothings seems to gets them going.
(7) They show emotional coldness, detachment, or flattened emotionality. The ultimate cold fish.

3. Schizotypal Personality Disorder

Here, managers are marked by acute discomfort with, and reduced capacity for, close relationships. They show many eccentricities of behaviour. They may look odd and have a reputation for being 'peculiar'.

(1) They have very odd ideas about business: how to succeed, who to hire, what controls what.
(2) They can have odd beliefs or magical thinking that influences behaviour

and is inconsistent with business norms, e.g. superstitiousness, belief in clairvoyance, telepathy. They get into crystals, feng shui and such like, in a very big and serious way.

(3) They can have odd thinking and speech styles, being very vague or very elaborate. They can seem 'other-worldly' and maybe very difficult to follow.

(4) They can have unusual perceptual experiences – seeing things that are not there, smell and taste things differently.

(5) Some are very suspicious or paranoid around the home and the office.

(6) They show inappropriate or constricted affect, they react oddly, emotionally in various contexts. That is, they may become very emotional around some trivial issues but strangely and unpredictably cold at others.

4. Antisocial Personality Disorder

These managers show a disregard for, and violation of, the rights of others. They often have a history of being difficult, delinquent or dangerous.

(1) They show a failure to conform to social norms with respect to lawful behaviours (repeatedly performing acts that are grounds for arrest, imprisonment and serious detention). This includes lying, stealing and cheating.

(2) They are always deceitful, as indicated by repeated lying, use of aliases, or conning others for personal profit or pleasure. They are nasty, aggressive, con artists – the sort who often get profiled on business crime programmes.

(3) They are massively impulsive and fail to plan ahead. They live only in, and for, the present.

(4) They show irritability and aggressiveness, as indicated by repeated physical fights or assaults. They can't seem to keep still – ever.

(5) They manifest a terrifying reckless disregard for the physical and psychological safety of self or others – or the business in general.

(6) They are famous for being consistently irresponsible. Repeated failure to sustain consistent work behaviour or to honour financial obligations are their hallmark.

(7) Most frustrating of all, they show lack of remorse. They are indifferent to, or rationalise, having hurt, mistreated, or stolen from another. They never learn from their mistakes. It can seem like labelling them as anti-social is a serious understatement.

5. Borderline Personality Disorder

These poor souls show chronic instability of interpersonal relationships, self-image, and emotion. They are also marked by impulsiveness in their daily behaviour.

(1) Sometimes they show frantic efforts to avoid real or imagined abandonment by managers, their staff, etc. They can become dependent and clinging.
(2) They often show a pattern of unstable and intense interpersonal relationships characterised by alternating between extremes of love and hate; worship and detestation.
(3) Most have identity disturbance – markedly and persistently unstable self-image or sense of self. They are not really sure who they are and assumed identity can easily change.
(4) They are impulsive with money, sex, booze, driving and so on, and in every sense of the word are accident-prone. They might spend lavishly the one day and be miserly the next.
(5) At extremes, they can show recurrent suicidal behaviour, or threats.
(6) Most noticeable is their marked change of mood (e.g. intense episodic dysphoria, irritability, or anxiety usually lasting a few hours and only rarely more than a few days). They seem to be on an emotional roller coaster with ups and downs, even in the same day.
(7) They often talk about chronic feelings of inner emptiness.
(8) Unfortunately for their reports and managers, they have inappropriate, intense anger or difficulty controlling anger (e.g. frequent displays of temper, constant anger, recurrent physical fights).

6. Histrionic Personality Disorder

These managers have excessive emotionality and attention seeking. They are the 'drama-queens' of the business world.

(1) Most are uncomfortable in situations in which they are not the centre of attention and try always to be so. They delight in making a drama out of a crisis.
(2) Their interaction with others is often characterised by inappropriate sexually seductive or provocative behaviour. Needless to say this causes more of a reaction in women than men.
(3) They display rapidly shifting and shallow expression of emotions. They are difficult to read.
(4) Most use physical appearance (clothes) to draw attention to self but this may include body piercing or tattooing. They certainly get a reputation in the office for their 'unique apparel'.

(5) Many have a style of speech that is excessively impressionistic and lacking in detail.
(6) Always they show self-dramatisation, theatricality, and exaggerated expression of emotion – usually negative. Even the dullest topic is imbued with drama.
(7) They are easily influenced by others or circumstances – and therefore both unpredictable and persuadable.
(8) Many consider relationships to be more intimate than they actually are. Being rather dramatic, they feel humdrum working relationships more intensely than others.

7. Narcissistic Personality Disorder

This manager is marked by grandiosity (in fantasy or behaviour), need for admiration, and lack of empathy. Self-centred, selfish, egotistical: they are everywhere in business – alas.

(1) They have a grandiose sense of self-importance (e.g. exaggerated achievements and talents, expectation to be recognised as superior without commensurate achievements).
(2) Most are preoccupied with fantasies of unlimited success, power, brilliance and money.
(3) They believe that they are 'special' and unique and can only be understood by, or should associate with, other special or high-status people (or institutions). They may try to 'buy' themselves into exclusive circles.
(4) Always they require excessive admiration and respect from everyone at work.
(5) Bizarrely, often they have a sense of entitlement, i.e. unreasonable expectations of especially favourable treatment or automatic compliance with their manifest needs.
(6) Worse, they take advantage of others to achieve their own ends, which makes them terrible managers.
(7) They lack empathy. All are unwilling to recognise or identify with the feelings and needs of others. They have desperately low EQ.
(8) Curiously they are often envious of others and believe that others are envious of them.
(9) They show arrogant, haughty behaviours or attitudes all the time and everywhere at work (and home). At times this can be pretty amusing but is mostly simply frustrating.

8. Avoidant Personality Disorder

These poor souls show social inhibition, feelings of inadequacy, and hypersensitivity to negative evaluation. They are super-sensitive, delicate flowers.

(1) They avoid occupational activities that involve significant interpersonal contact, because of fears of criticism, disapproval, or rejection. Any chance of negative feedback is to be avoided.
(2) They are unwilling to get involved with people unless certain of being liked which is pretty difficult at work – indeed anywhere.
(3) They show restraint within intimate relationships because of the fear of being shamed or ridiculed. They are cold fish.
(4) They seem always preoccupied with being criticised or rejected in work situations.
(5) They are inhibited in new interpersonal situations because of feelings of inadequacy.
(6) They see themselves as socially inept, personally unappealing, or inferior to others. It can be puzzling to wonder how they ever became managers in the first place. Certainly low self-esteem people rarely make it to the top in business.

9. Dependent Personality Disorder

These managers have a pervasive and excessive need to be taken care of by others. This leads to submissive and clinging behaviour and fears of separation.

(1) These managers suffer analysis paralysis. They can't make decisions on their own without continual advice and reassurance from others.
(2) They need others to assume responsibility for most major areas of their life. Inevitably they are good at delegating. But they seem always to need help and reassurance.
(3) Most have difficulty expressing disagreement with others because of fear of loss of support or approval. They publicly agree while privately disagreeing. This of course makes them difficult to read.
(4) They all have difficulty initiating projects or doing things on their own (because of a lack of self-confidence in judgement or abilities rather than a lack of motivation or energy). So they resist change, particularly where it leads to their being isolated or threatened.
(5) Some go to excessive lengths to obtain nurture and support from others often humiliating themselves in the process.

(6) All feel uncomfortable or helpless when alone because of exaggerated fears of being unable to care for themselves at work (and home).

10. Obsessive Compulsive Personality Disorder

These managers show a preoccupation with orderliness, perfectionism, and mental and interpersonal control, at the expense of flexibility, openness, and efficiency. They make for the most anal of bureaucrats.

(1) Always they are preoccupied with details, rules, lists, order, organisation, or schedules to the extent that the major point of the business activity is lost and forgotten.
(2) All show perfectionism that interferes with task completion (e.g. they are unable to complete a project because their own overly strict standards are not met). And of course they demand it in others however unproductive it makes them.
(3) These managers are often workaholics often excluding leisure activities and friendships. They are seriously driven workaholics.
(4) They have a well-deserved reputation for being overconscientious, scrupulous, and inflexible about matters of morality, ethics, or values.
(5) Amazingly, they are unable to discard worn-out or worthless objects even when they have no sentimental value. They hoard rubbish.
(6) They are reluctant to delegate tasks or to work with others unless they submit to exactly their way of doing things. They don't let go and pay the price.
(7) They are misers towards both themselves and others; money is viewed as something to be hoarded for future catastrophes. Because they never fully spend their budget, they never get it increased.
(8) In short, they show rigidity and stubbornness – very unpleasant to work for.

The personality disorders provide a good start for understanding a managerial madness. In this sense, some managers are genuinely mad – at least in the psychotic sense – and this accounts for their failure.

There are very important points to be made when looking at these personality disorders. It helps to explain why some organisations seem to select mad managers. Many of the predominant characteristics of the personality orders are, in moderation, often desirable in business. Narcissistic managers have plenty of self-esteem and can inspire confidence.

The obsessive compulsiveness of that disorder can be ideal for businesses that require careful checking or monitoring. Too little or too much of these traits can cause derailment.

Hogan (2000) took the personality disorders, translated them into everyday language and described how they measured the 'dark side' of the personality. His thesis is that there are both positive (strengths) and negative (shortcomings) facets of each of these disorders. A limited amount of each can be a strength. However too much is clearly a weakness.

	Factor	Strengths	Shortcomings
1.	**Excitable**	Empathy and concern	Emotional explosiveness
2.	**Sceptical**	Social and political insight	Excessive suspicion
3.	**Cautious**	Evaluates risks appropriately	Indecisiveness and risk aversion
4.	**Reserved**	Emotionally unflappable	Insensitive and poor communicator
5.	**Leisurely**	Good social skills	Passive aggression
6.	**Bold**	Courage and energy	Overbearing and manipulative
7.	**Mischievous**	Unafraid of risk	Reckless and deceitful
8.	**Colourful**	Celebrations and entertainment	Impulsive and distractible
9.	**Imaginative**	Creativity and vision	`Bad ideas
10.	**Diligent**	Hard work and high standards	Micromanagement
11.	**Dutiful**	Corporate citizenship	Indecisiveness

Table 1 – Strengths and Shortcomings of our Derailment Factors

McCall (1999) had a similar idea, noting that competencies can have a darker side.

Competency	Potential Dark Side
Team Player	Not a risk taker, indecisive, lacks independent judgement
Customer-Focused	Can't create breakthroughs, can't control costs, unrealistic, too conservative
Biased toward Action	Reckless, dictatorial
Analytic Thinker	Analysis paralysis, afraid to act, inclined to create large staffs
Has Integrity	Holier than thou attitude, rigid, imposes personal standards on others, zealots
Innovative	Unrealistic, impractical, wastes time and money
Has Global Vision	Misses local markets, over-extended, unfocused
Good with People	Soft, can't make tough decisions, too easy on people

Table 2 – Competencies and their Dark Side

The idea then is that any human characteristic – normal or pathological – can, in excess, be a weakness. There is no linear relationship between these characteristics and success or failure. Most managers believe that one cannot get enough of certain characteristics like intelligence or integrity or innovativeness and they are sought out largely by selectors. They then become puzzled when their star managers derail.

C – Sad Management

There is something poignant about the discarded technology of another era. Graveyards of old cars, old typewriters, old records are memorials of a time that will not return. They certainly had their day: once they were cutting edge, state-of-the-art. But like towns that have withered when the gold ran out or the highway was diverted, they are simply sad reminders of what once was. Some managers are sad cases for the same reason. Life, technology and the new ways have left them marooned on a foreign shore. Like all those communist leaders in a post-communist world, they are merely sad reminders of a distant past – another time – when they were useful.

Sad managers can't quite hack it. They don't have the competency for the job. They are sadly lacking. Consider the following list of competencies and how sad managers just do not have them.

The quest for definitive, comprehensive, universal 'periodic table' of competencies has continued. For instance Dulewicz (1989) is convinced that there are 12 'totally independent' dimensions of performance or key supra-competencies derived from 49 primary competencies. The behaviour of sad managers is contrasted with these competencies.

Intellectual

Strategic perspective

☑ Rises above the detail so see the broader issues and implications; takes account of wide-ranging influences and situations both inside and outside the organisation before planning or acting.

☒ The sad manager is organocentric; inwardly focused; often not even tactical let alone strategic. They can't see the wood for the trees and have no clear idea what strategy is.

Analysis and judgement

☑ Seeks all relevant information; identifies problems, relates relevant data, and identifies causes; assimilates numerical data accurately and makes sensible interpretations; work is precise and methodical, and relevant detail is not overlooked. Makes decisions based on logical assumptions that reflect factual information.

☒ Sad managers are often not bright enough to be analytic, using superstition more than data analysis to make decisions, or are perhaps just decision avoidant.

Planning and organisation

☑ Plans priorities, assignments and the allocation of resources; organises resources efficiently and effectively, delegating work to the appropriate staff.

☒ The sad are badly organised; not quite just-in-time, habitually late managers. They can't or won't plan and are often famous for it.

Managing staff

☑ Adopts appropriate styles for achieving group objectives; monitors and evaluates their work; shows vision and inspiration; develops the skills and competencies of staff.

☒ Sad managers set no targets, manage neither by objectives nor goals and rarely appraise. Their staff are neither punished nor rewarded and soon become alienated and unproductive. Management is about setting clear, attainable but stretchable goals and targets; and supporting others in achieving these. Sad managers can and do neither.

Persuasiveness

☑ Influences and persuades others to give their agreement and commitment; in face of conflict, uses personal influence to communicate proposals, to reach bases for compromise and to reach an agreement.

☒ Sad managers have little charm or influence. They are as likely to be passive aggressive as assertive. They are famous for their inability to get their way except by threats and force.

Assertiveness and decisiveness

☑ Ascendant and forceful dealing with others; can take charge; willing to take risks and seek new experiences; decisive, ready to take decisions, even on limited information.

☒ It is around these issues that sad managers are at their most observable. They are ditherers, conflict averse and risk avoiding. Indeed, they themselves should be avoided. They delay, prevaricate and procrastinate and may be famous for their inability to make even simple decisions.

Interpersonal sensitivity

☑ Shows consideration for the needs and feelings of others; listen dispassionately, is not selective, recalls key points and takes account of them; is flexible when dealing with others, will change own position when others' proposals warrant it.

☒ In short, sad managers have low EQ; possess little insight or counselling skills. They cannot read others and are not sensitive, nor are they flexible because they are quite unable to adapt to emotional situations.

Oral communication

☑ Fluent, speaks clearly and audibly, with good diction; in formal presentations, is enthusiastic and lively, tailors content to audience's level of understanding.

☒ Sad managers are often shy, incoherent and inarticulate.

Adaptability

Adaptability and resilience

☑ Adapts behaviour to new situations; resilient, maintains effectiveness in face of adversity or unfairness. Performance remains stable when under pressure or opposition; does not become irritable and anxious, retains composure.

☒ Sad managers buckle under pressure; have few good coping mechanisms and have a tendency towards hypochondria.

Results Orientation

☑ Energy and initiative; makes a strong, positive impression, has authority and credibility; is a self-starter and originator, actively influences events to achieve goals; has energy and vitality, maintains high level of activity and produces a high level of output.

☒ Passive, with low wattage, the sad manager is slow, reactive and conformist. They seem to run out of steam very easily and to be more happily reacting to situations than planning ahead.

Achievement-motivation

☑ Sets demanding goals for self and for others, and is dissatisfied with average performance; makes full use of own time and resources; sees a task through to completion, irrespective of obstacles and setbacks.

☒ Sad managers coast rather than push. It seems as if everything is 'just too much' for them – they certainly do not evidence much drive, thrust or need to win. Few are self-starters; none is driven.

Business sense

☑ Identifies opportunities that will increase sales or profits; selects and exploits those activities that will result in the largest return. Business sense is like common sense in that many people believe, quite erroneously that they have business sense in droves.

☒ Bad managers have neither common sense nor business sense. They probably never had either or will acquire it.

Source: 'Assessment centres as the route to competence', B.Dulewicz, Personal Management, November 1989, pp. 56-59.

Sad managers are incompetent and they derail. They may once have been competent in a different age and a different environment, but have failed to adapt to the future. Or they may have never, ever been competent and were appointed to their position by incompetent selectors or those motivated by corruption. On the other hand, it is possible that they were 'super competent' and that lead to their failure. Thus they may have been too strategic and never tactical; too analytical and thus too slow; too eager to plan and too slow to act, and so on.

In his analysis of the derailment literature, Hogan (2000) found similarity between three studies each of which tried to specify the facts of managerial failure (see Table 3).

Bentz	**McCall & Lombardo**	**Lombardo, Ruderman & McCauley**
Lack of business knowledge Lack of business skill	Specific business problems Unable to think strategically	Handling business complexity
Failure of leadership	Over- and under-managing Not staffing effectively	Directing, motivating & developing subordinates
Failure to shape events	Specific performance problems	Drive for excellence
Lack of administrative skill	Overly ambitious	Savvy
Poor judgement Overriding personality defect	Social insensitivity	Sensitivity
Inability to deal with scope and scale	Failing to staff effectively	Staffing

Table 3 – Comparative results of Three Studies of Managerial Derailment

Six are listed, and are perfectly compatible with the idea of bad, mad and sad managers.

A

Appraisal apologetics

Students of divinity used to be taught, and maybe still are, a course called Christian Apologetics. Its content is usually a close examination and rebuttal of arguments against Christianity. Thus one examines the Freudian, Humanist and Marxist argument and how the theologians have come back at their detractors. The Jesuits, those shock troops of the Catholic Church, are particularly well inoculated against doubters, debates and debasers by years of training in the casuistry and sophistry of apologetics.

Perhaps the poor, ever-attached HR manager trying to instal a good appraisal scheme needs the same treatment. We know that nearly all people both agree that appraisal is a good idea principle but that their particular system doesn't work. Try introducing any appraisal system and one is faced by an army of those trying to stop it from the passive, aggressive snipers, to the openly hostile who try, often successfully, to derail the process.

There are of course many reasons why people are hostile to appraisal. But the most common is the fear of being 'smoked out' through being explicitly compared on objective criteria. The stakes are high for the less successful and they can mount a powerful attack that needs a good defence.

Consider the following ten objections and their possible rebuttal.

1. *Once-a-year (or even twice) critiquing (at the annual appraisal) encourages people to save up and squirrel away both praise and criticism for months instead of giving it at the appropriate time.* This is very rare: the difference in the appraisal is that it is detailed, numeric,

generic and comparative. Day-to-day feedback that is specific and immediate is necessary and the sign of a good manager. The two are related but different.

2. *Managers are cowardly: they know low marks are demoralising so they avoid (justly) giving them and hence a paper trail of the poor performers suggests they are performing well.* This is certainly true and perhaps the greatest cause of appraisal system failure, but it can be cured by a mixture of rater training and rewards for managers who give honest feedback. Using a 'forced distribution' where raters have to use the whole scale (so many 5, 4, 3, 2, 1 points) leads to too many problems. Manager pusilanimousness is a human failing not exclusively an appraisal issue.

3. *Appraisal confounds different functions: feedback, coaching, development, pay decisions, legal documentation.* It can, but it need not. It is about detailed feedback. It can be used to generate numbers for pay and promotion decisions but it does not have to. It is never sufficient for any coaching though may play an integral part of it. Best to separate pay and appraisal at first so that it is not seen exclusively as a remuneration exercise.

4. *Appraisal is evaluation by ambush because employees were encouraged to meet a standard they had not seen, understood or thought relevant to their job.* This is only the case if appraisal systems are not properly piloted or introduced. In fact the precise opposite is most often the case – people complain about being over-consulted by HR over the contents of the appraisal form with which they are all too familiar.

5. *Appraisals are either too inflexible to force real differentiation between individuals on trivial criteria, or else so specific that no useful comparative data is generated.* Certainly the size and complexity of the organisation can make comparisons difficult: the accountant, the engineer and the marketing manager do different jobs. But there are two ways round this. First everyone beyond a certain level (say supervisor) can be evaluated on the competencies that HR specialists spent such a lot of energy drawing up, describing and explaining which are considered to embody the unique and important features of the whole organisation (vision, mission, blah/blah). The second approach is to allow unique and shared criteria: the former called personal goals or key

result areas; the latter comparing competencies or management practices. These can count fifty-fifty so that people are rated on both unique and comparable criteria – very common, pretty simple.

6. *The Appraisal system is not organisation-wide; special groups opt out quite unreasonably and unfairly.* This does happen paradoxically most often with the top board who are supposed to model and endorse it. Lots of specialists also make a bold attempt to be excluded on the grounds of being unique. But if they are allowed to get away with it, the system is really not a system for the company.

7. *Appraising and giving feedback is a skill that needs to be taught before any system is put in place, i.e. the system is not supported by training.* This may be true but does not have to be. Time, effort and money are needed in three phases: system design, implementation and maintenance. Training is part of the latter two where both energy and money are low. The low EQ manager desperately needs training but everyone does, to ensure people know the theory and practice of appraisal.

8. *The rating scale means the numbers and the words do not match.* This is an important issue that can be unsolvable. Most rating scales used in appraisal are five point scales with verbal description, i.e. 1 = under performance; 2 = marginal; 3 = satisfactory; 4 = above average; 5 = excellent performance. It is a recipe for disaster. It turns into a 3 or 2 point scale that effectively does not differentiate the good and the bad. What psychometricians know is that the best scales, if you want differentiation, are (like the gates of hell) even. Thus an eight or ten point scale is best. Even scales prevent fence-sitting. And they are not necessarily accompanied by verbal tables. The problem is this: the difference between *slightly* and *moderately*, and *moderately* and *very*, and *very* and *exceptionally* is not necessarily the same. But the difference between 3 and 4, is the same as that between 5 and 6 or 6 and 7. In statistical jargon, the problem is having different scales: normal, ordinal, interval and ratio. But managers demand words to explain numbers and this is the beginning of the end. There are not enough words to adequately describe performance on a differentiating scale. The scales are wide, even and anchored at both ends like **Unacceptable Performance 1 2 3 4 5 6 7 8 9 10 Exceptional Performance.** If a dim and difficult manager demands

some words saying he or she does know the difference between a 5 and 6, say the answer is 1. Verbal descriptors in a short, uneven, scale are a sure recipe for failure.

9. *A cost-benefit analysis of designing, implementing and maintain a PMS implies frankly it is not worth it.* Not all systems require months of super-consultant time and expense but they must not be amateur. Paradoxically, it is the effort put in maintaining a system rather than designing it, that is most important to ensure its success.

10. *Individual appraisal ruins teamwork and team spirit.* Most organisations talk a good game on teamwork but because all this collectivist stuff is deeply counter-cultural, we send contradictory messages. Traditionally, appraisal is done on an individual basis: it's the individual's style, effort and outcome that are appraised not the team that they are in, if indeed they are. But that need not be the case. It is perfectly simple to institute team assessment and appraisal if that is really wanted.

In the old days, Marxists used to be annoyed when their opponents pointed to the incompetence, inefficiency and downright evil in states that proudly bore the name of Marx. Russia and China they argued were not really Marxist at all. They did not follow the theory. They were ideologically impure. Their practice did not follow the true ideology and therefore could, and should, not be allowed to attack it.

The same is true for apologists of appraisal. To point out innumerable examples of where high sums of money and energy resulted only in bickering demonstrated staff does not mean appraisal in unnecessary or demotivating. They simply did not do it right. And they are right to do so. It can work well. And as the blessed Margaret used to say: 'There is no alternative!'

Analysing your boss

Most managers want to know how to manage certain of those more problematic staff: the chronic dissenter; the demotivated clock-watcher; Job's comforter; the neurotically fragile. A great deal of time and effort, energy and worry go into trying to understand and motivate direct reports to be productive.

But the really smart manager spends as much time managing upwards. By definition, your boss has greater power and status than you. Bosses may or may not have broader wisdom and more experience but (nearly) always they have more power and influence and certainly more command of resources. They certainly are likely to have a great influence on your promotability, bonus pay and, indeed, quality of life.

Really shrewd managers learn to handle their bosses. The success of this strategy depends entirely on an understanding of the individual concerned. And this is much trickier than understanding reporting staff because managers mostly have much more data on those below them than those above them. Often, managers chose their direct reports; they have access to their files; they may even have valuable psychometric test information on their personality and motives. They certainly have much more daily contact with them. The quality and quantity of data that managers have is often extensive, while a remote (physically or psychologically) boss may be very difficult to know. Managers probably have up to 50 times more contact with their staff than with the bosses who maybe in a different building, city, even country.

But what are individual bosses really like? What are their ambitions and values? Who do they most admire or loathe in the organisation? How do they manage upwards? And what pressures are they under? What rewards do they most value – promotion, bonuses, education, time off? What gives them most stress? Are they themselves high flyers or ceiling reachers? Are they totally trustworthy? And, even, are they sane?

A simple but effective way to begin managing upwards is to understand the abilities and personality of one's manager.

A – Ability

How bright is your boss? Ignore qualification, rank and reputation. In assessing bosses, the question to ask is how fast they are on the uptake? How quickly and accurately can they comprehend a report? How good is their vocabulary, written skills and articulateness? Can they 'tumble-numbers', read a balance sheet? The real test is in the unfamiliar, not the familiar. It's called fluid intelligence. Experience leads to crystallised knowledge, but is only really useful in a stable world.

Those with bright bosses (that's IQ not EQ) may find them a little intolerant of those less quick and perhaps poor at explanation. Reminding them of this can be done in a flattering way and may help everybody. These bright sparks tend to be more accepting of change, more interested in data and, of course, more adaptable and flexible.

Below-par bosses may take particularly sensitive handling. They resist new ideas and are frightened of bright young things from university. The really dim ones don't even know that they are dim. They need a lot of help and support. Give them 'suggestions' and show them how to do things. But don't make them too reliant on you – they may hold on to you too hard and prevent your progress if they need you too much.

B – Personality

There are essentially five personality traits that require close attention. The first is perhaps the most tricky and almost a taboo to talk about. It's **neuroticism** or, if you prefer, 'negative affectivity'. The stable boss copes with stress well, but the neurotic boss can be anxious, moody, thin-skinned, touchy and brittle, always pessimistic and worrying. Neurotic bosses are often unpredictable and need constant help, reassurance and calming down. They can have self-defeating characteristics that need looking out for, lest they defeat you as well. Neurotics are supersensitive – to the environment and others' feelings. In that sense, they can be very compassionate, but their sensitivity makes them prone to low self-esteem, guilt, hypochondria, even obsessiveness.

The best way to manage these bosses for you own mental health is frankly to leave them. The cost of being a part-time therapist may be simply too high a price to pay.

The second important characteristic is **extroversion**. Extroverts are active, expressive, impulsive and sociable. They can also be risk taking, showing a worrying lack of reflection and responsibility. They are prone to make mistakes; to trade off speed for accuracy; to have too many brainstorming groups and parties; and to search for the elusive breakthrough. Extroverts need not have their enthusiasm dimmed, but they need watching. They need to have their impulsiveness tempered by more considerate judgment. But they also need lots of stimulation and variety to keep them comfortable.

Introverts are not shy, inadequate: they just don't have the need for excitement that extroverts show. They tend to be more difficult to read because they prefer not to go to parties or meetings or give talks. They think first, speak later (unlike extroverts, who do it the other way around), and may seem slow and ponderous. They may seem cold, but that is just their discomfort around others.

Introverts trade off speed for accuracy. They may be helped by having an extroverted spokesperson. They prefer listening to talking and have a preference for 'cold' over 'hot' media: they prefer letters to meetings; emails to brainstorming sessions. Understand their likes and dislikes and you become more trusted and liked yourself.

We all like our managers to be **conscientious**: to be efficient, organised, reliable, responsible, dependent, thorough and prudent. Often they make the same demands of us, which can be a little exacting. But they get things done. Conscientiousness is a predictor of business success. It comes from upbringing and values. It is related to the work ethic and one's conscience.

Conscientious managers can be rather tight-fisted and intolerant and they can be risk-adverse. But beware imprudent managers. They are lax with time, money and their personal responsibilities to others. They don't follow through. They don't pay their bills and they can be wildly incautious about all monetary and security issues. They may take time off when it suits them and be both indulgent and impulsive. They may appear as if they feel that 'The problem with instant gratification is that it takes too long.'

An imprudent, unreliable manager needs watching. They need lots of backup – but ultimately they probably need managing out of the organisation, for everyone's benefit.

The fourth personality dimension of salience is **agreeableness**. Highly agreeable managers are lovely: they are appreciative, forgiving, generous, kind, trusting and sympathetic. Their staff experience them as altruistic, modest and straightforward. Needless to say, they are well liked and have a reputation for being good managers.

Those low on agreeableness are much less likeable. They may be cynical and sarcastic, argumentative and challenging, inconsiderate, suspicious and unhelpful. They tend to want to be admired and to be 'somebody'. Their vanity and habit of putting people down make them unloved, unrespected and quite simply disagreeable. If their disagreeability is matched by great abilities, they may be forgiven their unkindnesses. But it is more likely that disagreeable managers get where they are through lies, nepotism or exploitation. If any of the latter, the best strategy is to leave or get them out of the way.

The fifth personality dimension of importance is one clearly related to creativity and intellect. It's called **openness to experience**. Managers who score high on this dimension tend to be artistic and curious, imaginative and insightful, original and creative. Typically, they have a wide range of interests and are quite 'intellectual'. Often, they are thought of as unconventional and a bit 'arty-farty'. They like variety and novelty, but can scatter resources. For some, they are impractical dreamers: optimistic, energetic but unfocused.

Open managers are not fuddy-duddy. They embrace changes and are sensitive to the teachings and ideas of others. They are also aesthetically sophisticated. Some jobs call for little imagination and in those they are a handicap. But the real pains are managers who score low on this dimension. They tend to express both discomfort and perplexity in reaction to novel experiences. Their rigidity and lack of curiosity can be misunderstood as resistance. To help the less open manager, one needs to provide practical suggestions and new ideas. He or she needs to be helped to be more attentive to what is going on around them. They have an impoverished fantasy life and very conventional ways of thinking and behaving. Those scoring very low on this dimension are very hostile to new ideas, but those mid-way may come really to appreciate the new ways of thinking that you feed them.

If you have a bright, stable, agreeable, conscientious and open boss, celebrate your good fortune. If not, start practising you upward management skills!

Arbeit Zeitgeist

Cynics say that business school dons are really merely business historians because all they can really understand and explain is the past. Library shelves are full of padded-out business books predicting both miracles and catastrophes that never happened.

Manically optimistic, South-Sea-bubblers predicted a whole new web world that created overnight multi-millionaires. A few lone voices of scepticism were ridiculed as fuddy-duddies worthy of only contempt. But now we know better.

Business gurus are fond of contrasting the past with the present. They draw a picture based on hearsay, guesswork and the presentational imperative of having slides which show dramatic opposites. Sparse evidence is cited to justify the contrast effects. And those who remember business in the 50s or 60s, or indeed read the literature of that time, are quick to challenge the description of the era. Others are equally unhappy about a description of the present that they have personally never witnessed.

It's safest sticking to futurology: you don't need any data and can speak with messianic certainty. Optimism sells, not pessimism, so the future at work is full of labour-saving devices, instant communication and smooth, bureaucracy-free transactions.

But even the futurologists can't resist the compare and contrast model – the past vs. the present vs. the future. And they tend to pick out specific features of the business. In the old days, things were slow, safe and provincial. It was a time of certainty, but also prejudice. 'Stale, pale, males', as they are now called, were in charge; women did not feature in management and the labour force was prepared to endure monotonous jobs in the same company all its working life.

The hind-sighters saw the fifties and sixties as a time when there were rigid hierarchies. A time when there were different levels of dining area: senior dining room for the board, the management mess and the workers' canteen. We are meant to look back with a mixture of disbelief and disgust that people could be so snobbish, petty and trivial. Of course it's not like that now!

Or is it just more subtle? The zeitgeist might call for more democracy, flatter organisations, teamwork and so on, but have bosses simply not become more astute in hiding their privileges? Some organisations have been flattened during kaisen-based restructuring exercises, but the question is, when did organisations begin to get tall, hierarchical, and whatever?

Next we are told that all reward structures were service-orientated, not performance-orientated. That is, in the old days, promotion came with length of service, irrespective of the quality of the service. People gained experience through service, which was the basic requirement for managerial promotion.

Today we are told that all businesses have performance management systems, which ensure that it is measured performance on the job that determines salary increases and promotion. But try finding a handful of companies with a well built, accepted and functioning performance management system. Or locating companies where there is not a fairly strong relationship between age and seniority. It is a difficult task.

The hype is about performance; the reality is still about service. Even young people don't buy the idea of working for companies for three to five year stretches throughout a working lifetime in order to build up a portfolio of experience.

The fifties and sixties, and even more the seventies, are seen as a time of confrontations. It was management against unions; of us vs. them; of 'I'm all right Jack'. It was an era of restricted practices; of jobsworth attitudes; of intolerance.

Certainly union power and numbers have decreased. Organised protest is much less evidence. 'Walk-outs', 'sit-ins' and all that mayhem from seventies' manufacturing and mining sectors seems a long time ago and best forgotten. Mrs Thatcher, some argue, cured the British disease, by de-industrialising the country and ignoring the unions.

Just as status-consciousness and hierarchy are currently merely more hidden, so it seems the psychology that drove old-fashioned confrontations has now simply been individualised. Passed-over-and-pissed-off employees now do not join the union for retribution or vengeance. They simply try alternative means: whistle-blowing, stealing, sabotage, selling secrets. The growth of the latter activities has truly been remarkable and could be seen as old-fashioned strikes in their modern guise.

There are all sorts of other then-and-now dimensions that seem pretty dodgy. The past – that is the working environments of the 50s and 60s is seen as safe, steady and boring. There was little or no innovation, job stress or real work ethic. Those that lived through these times may well be surprised by this revelation.

The 60s were a time of unprecedented change. Vietnam, retreat from empire, civil liberties, a man-on-the-moon were dominant features. The oil crisis dominated the 70s. And they ended with perhaps the most radical de-industrialisation in this country's history under Margaret Thatcher.

It's just too easy to believe we exclusively live in interesting times. Optimists over- estimate our progress; pessimists our stress. The truth is, too many features of work endure across generations.

B

Business escatology: Future optimists and pessimists

In theological terms, **escatology** is the doctrine(s) of 'things to come'. And for those who abhor ambiguity, casuistry or sophistry, there are two very clear opposites: hell-fire, eternal damnation and the dubious joys of meeting Beelzebub, or relishing the angelic choirs, Elysium and paradise (for ever) with the Almighty.

This life is a preparation for the next. Where you go (up or down in 'Otis-Escatology') is a function of how you spend your time, squander your talents, treat your fellow humankind. All of us get our just desserts. And we make choices that determine our outcomes. Where you end up is not due to chance, fate or capricious forces beyond your comprehension, control or prediction. There are many long religious handbooks that dictate how you should behave to end up among the righteous. But the temptations of the flesh too are many.

In the last century, before the Western Churches appeared to have abolished personal responsibility for sin (let alone original sin), preachers found the best way both to convert and maintain believers was to preach hell-fire. Eternal damnation was not just nothingness; not even separation from the Almighty; it was quite literally hell. The idea seemed so horrid that most tried religious observance as insurance policy.

Hell-fire-and-damnation preachers relied on the push rather than the pull factor. One was not pulled by the joys of heaven but pushed by the vision of the fires of hell.

What has all this theological language got to do with business? Well, think of the Millennium Bug: surely the cleverest piece of IT scaremongering ever invented. Were they not the hell-fire predictors of today? Do you not recall the full meltdown we were promised by these doom merchants: planes falling out of the sky; nuclear power plants blowing up; computer records being erased? Employers would be trapped in lifts. All appliances would fail: the freezer would defrost; the central heating would not work; nor would your PC or your television.

Governments, companies, even individuals, took fright, threw money at the doomsday merchants and all was well. Then events became not unlike the story of the tribe that believed it had to sacrifice a virgin (daily) for the sun to rise. It was only when they ran out of virgins did they find their behaviour was pointless. This was because there were what scientists call 'control groups' over the millennium bug issue. The poor governments of Eastern Europe, supposedly most vulnerable to the bug, either did not know, care or could afford the prophylactic, but nothing much happened to them either.

Curiously the IT people are neither apologetic nor have they reformed. They are surprisingly like those believers in Armageddon who foretell the end of the world but when it goes wrong find plausible excuses only to change both the date and the means of destruction.

But one should not blame it all on IT people. How many talks has one heard about e-this, e-that, the web; the end of snail-mail; the high street and all the rest. The new world apparently consists of two types: the majority who sit at home by the pool, in the Jacuzzi, sipping Chardonnay, while doing banking, shopping, earning on their laptops. Precisely who is going to be the second type, whizzing round Waitrose shelves collecting, packing and delivering your order is not clear. That will never be fun – though of course part of it may be automated in the future.

So there will be the winners and the losers; the chosen and the damned; the harp players and the fire-stokers. The chosen will be wired, connected, literate and pampered; the damned will be the hewers of wood (IKEA) and drawers of water (sparkling Perrier). The chosen will log in; the damned will deliver.

Business escatologists are almost always in the fear business. Their favourite word is not *sin* but *change*. This is a remorseless, unstoppable, accelerating force that is the devil incarnate. The devil can only be placated by indulgences. We call these invoices and they too are remorseless and accelerating. They are given to those who can intercede for us to prevent destruction (of the business).

There seems almost no talk of heaven for business escatologists. A desert people see a water garden and oasis as heaven. Cold, crowded northerners see a palm-fringed tropical island abundant in all one's needs. What is heaven in business: continuous expansion, market share, profits – forever? Improbable, impossible – no selling point there.

But the opposite scenario is more clear, more likely and better known. Sudden stiff competition, industrial unrest, collapse of share price, profits turn to losses. The question becomes how to prevent that happening.

Optimism sounds naive; pessimism profound. So business escatology is about Armageddon – and how to avoid it. It is the scaremongery of the Victorian preachers and it works wonders.

Bond in the boardroom: Business espionage

Knowing all about your competitors is good business. Understanding business opponents' products and processes, sales figure and suppliers, capacity and customers as well as technology and staff training can really give a company the competitive edge. Insider knowledge gained at the right moment could be used to destroy, neutralise or fatally wound an enemy organisation – with the ultimate objective of becoming brand leader.

Hence the importance of business secrets and the efforts companies go to in protecting themselves against spies from the opposition. There are, as a result, all sorts of business myths, for instance that only a handful (literally) of chosen people know the secret formula for a certain product. It was once noted that only five (or three or seven – it does not matter) people know the part recipe for Coca-Cola and that they are never able to meet and are strictly forbidden from flying on the same plane. A likely story.

Certainly, the knowledge of ingredients and their amounts in certain unique products are worth protecting, but so is the manufacturing process. Companies also have favoured exclusive suppliers, loyal customers who receive special deals, and technologies which may be uniquely efficient – knowing how low-cost or innovative competitors do things is worth a great deal.

Lots of people other than market competitors are after company secrets. Financial journalists love a good scoop; pressure groups love a bit of 'third-world/environment/animals exploitation' material to help their boycott campaigns; investors, customers and even PhD students stand to gain from close-guarded information. And then there are the tax officials, the police and government departments who occasionally like to know what precisely is going on with certain companies' shady dealings. Hence we have a range of techniques, from the sophisticated to the sleazy, to spy on one's 'enemy'. Some are regarded as necessary business practice; others are downright illegal. All make good material for business ethics students to debate.

The methods can be simply divided into people vs. observational strategies and each involves different approaches.

1. People Methods

A. **Hiring competitor employees** with highly attractive packages. This means carefully targeting individuals 'in-the-know', who can be persuaded both to leave and 'spill the beans'. This is a difficult assignment: finding the right people, then knowing and providing what will make them leave. Expensive as a strategy, but potentially very successful. It is said that investment companies target top tax inspectors, thus turning the gamekeeper into the poacher.

B. **Conducting phoney job interviews.** This is a much cheaper (and dodgier) method. One simply advertises job vacancies, with very attractive specifications and packages, which actually don't exist. You then interview in depth only those from companies that have the secrets you need, before deciding that a 'restructuring leads the client to devote the job to other functions'. Time consuming, and rather naughty.

C. **Using trade fairs and conferences** to pick the brains of technical people. A couple of glasses of wine in a nice venue mean that one can flatter the knowledgeable 'techy' to give up many trade secrets just by being incredibly interested and attractive. A hint of sexual chemistry may help here!

D. **Using newspaper reports about company activities** of all types, one can target 'middle-managers' with interested calls. People who are unused to flattery are very vulnerable and may give up a lot of secrets. If the company has won an award, phone up to congratulate and ask them to speak at a local event to tell the story. If the company has had a lay-off or a drop in shares, do the same, but in commiseration. Powerful emotions lead the guard to drop, particularly in those not used to being in the limelight.

E. **Placing your people in their camp**. This means trying to get one of your employees to get a job in the opposition. Their primary aim while under your employ (they get paid twice), is to find out and relay the secrets. Very James Bond – important then to get the right chap for this sort of caper, which is long-term project.

2. Observation Methods

A. **Studying aerial photographs** of plants to which access is restricted. This can reveal plant layout (which is often a clue to process) inventory stockpiles, a tip-off for a sales drive, etc.

B. **Videotape comings and goings** to headquarters, plants etc. This can give information about who works, where and when. It can give clues about particular individuals, but also shift patterns, recruitment, downsizing etc.

C. **Reverse engineering**, which involves taking products apart to study components and manufacturing processes. Equally, a chemical analysis of the product can be performed to try to determine the ingredients and preparation method.

D. **Garbology**: obtaining the rubbish people throw away, examining everything including shredded papers. This is somewhere between post-modern archaeology and paparazzi low life, but it does reveal a great deal if one is (a) patient, (b) partial to rubber gloves and (c) desperately inquisitive.

Most of us have become used to living in a surveillance culture where cameras are everywhere. There are now specialist shops that advertise in airline magazines, that effectively sell espionage and counter-espionage equipment, miniature cameras, microphones and so on.

Some companies invest a lot of money and effort keeping their secrets. Others are more interested in getting the secrets of others. The reactive and proactive, defensive and offensive. The sector the company works in, its history and the paranoia or entrepreneurship of the CEO seem to dictate its attitude to business espionage rather than business ethics. But successful companies cannot afford to ignore their competitors. The only question is how they prefer to obtain their information.

Business Travel

The advertisements may make business travel look stylish, romantic, even exotic but the frequent business traveller knows otherwise. Yes – wider seats and booze-stocked lounges help, but there are the same delays, the same passport queries, the same lost luggage and the same jetlag. Many only know the journey from airport to hotel and back, never seeing anything else.

It is no accident that the words *travel* and *travail* are etymologically linked. Travel, at least the modern form of it, is just as likely to broaden the behind as it is the mind. It is said that the definition of a consultant is 'a simple organism designed to change bullshit into air miles'. But that is a bit old-hack now as air miles seem far less attractive then they once were.

A lot of travel-induced frustration comes from waiting around. Even if the absurdly detailed timetable is running smoothly, there is inevitably much hanging about: for transport to the airport, the check-in queue, the compulsory two-hour (and getting longer) margin. The shops may well be interesting, the business lounge comfortable, and the range of periodicals splendid, but still the business person is adrift in an unfamiliar environment.

For the 'little people', who travel 'at the back of the bus', the journey is not unlike a spell in prison. Airlines, like prisons, deprive the traveller of most of their belongings, reduce them to a number (64D, non-smoking); feed them bland fare when it suits the crew; and require undignified queuing for the lavatories. The hapless traveller is moved from one room to another for no apparent reason, and their papers and checked and re-checked by strict, no-nonsense members of staff. One is physically constrained in many senses, encouraged to remain strapped in, and required to share personal space with complete strangers. Ah yes, corralled, processed, drugged and dismissed: the four stages of the economy flight.

But flying is tiring and stressful at the best of times. Everyone gets jet lag; many people become dehydrated; and most lose sleep. A sizeable proportion of travellers actually have mild to serious bouts of flying anxiety. This can be acute, brought on by turbulence, or more debilitatingly chronic, which is difficult to cure. And now of course we have the terrorist scares. It is much worse than the 1970s when hijacking was relatively common because then most passenger hostages survived. Now planes are bombs and that New York scene is vividly imprinted on most people's minds. Travel is tiring, sure: but much, much worse, it looks very dangerous. Famous for being the safest means of transportation, it now seems the most perilous.

Business trips abroad are also expensive. Organisations realising the business traveller is a cash cow for hotels and airlines, charge preposterous amounts for simple services like faxes, meeting room space and so on. As a consequence, they have tried to reduce costs either by downgrading their executives or by trying to encourage them to do business over the Internet.

One central question is: is business travel really necessary? Does the face-to-face meeting have particular advantages over the videoconference, the e-mail, or whatever?

One should not assume that face-to-face is easier, more comfortable or more natural. One can feel bewildered and disoriented abroad. The helpless, hopeless, hapless traveller is not an uncommon sight at airports, shopping arcades and business conferences. There is a powerlessness about fear of loss of influence, and about the speed and outcome of one's business.

There is, too, the powerlessness of not knowing what is happening at home. The phone, fax and e-mail trilogy won't do. It becomes impossible to be fully functional in two places at once. And the more powerless one feels abroad, the more the fear of being left out at home grows. The astute traveller, therefore, details what information is to be passed on, when, and by whom, and pre-plans the mechanism to deal with incoming calls.

Doing business abroad is tiring because one needs to concentrate more. Foreigners, whatever their native tongue, do speak another language. Even first-language English speakers in other countries can have almost impenetrable accents, and use unknown acronyms and metaphors. The smattering of the language one learnt at school is often useless. 'Where is the hotel?', That is too expensive.' 'I need to check that with my colleagues' are far more useful phrases than those concerning the ubiquitous 'pen of my aunt'.

Foreign countries present problems; they do things differently there. And it is probably at the most trivial level that these differences cause headaches. The electrical appliances are different. The tipping system is impenetrable. They don't take all your credit cards. All the concentration and adaptation lead quickly to fatigue. Bereft of the familiar comforts of home, overfed, overwatered and overstimulated, one can soon be tempted to behave like a fractious child. Capricious, irascible moods do not lead to fruitful or beneficial business. But they can be guarded against by a little preparation and quite reasonable demands for 'time out' from the frantic socialising and business activities. Sleep, exercise and cultural homework are better ways to use down time than in-house movies or a bender at the mini-bar.

Paradoxically, it is the after, rather than the during, work activities with the natives that prove most difficult because of all the subtle cultural differences. Many behavioural norms and niceties are passed on by 'old hands', and can be found in books. The importance of gifts in the Far East is well known as is the idea that, whereas Americans like to socialise (casually) after a deal, the Japanese do so before. Many social traditions are bewildering; it is easy to be bored or boring, vulgar and rude, insensitive or garish, by misreading the signals or assuming that everyone is a PLU (person like us).

So if business travel is tiring, expensive and dangerous, what are the options? First there are a few distinctions to be made about what sort of communication is required.

1. Is the purpose a one-to-one (or series of) meetings or are many people (committee) involved at the same time?
2. Are all parties communicating in a language they feel competent and comfortable in?
3. Have they met before or at least do they have a reasonable understanding of each other's countries?

Clearly one-to-one meetings with people speaking the same language and with cultural familiarity are easier. The problem lies in the opposite pattern. The question then becomes the advantages and disadvantages of the medium of communication.

We now have various options.

1. Video-conferencing – where one has close assimilation of face-to-face communication, all the non-verbal bodily communication cues.
2. Telephone – where one has vocal and verbal cues, the words, accent, voice quality.
3. E-mail – where one only has verbal cues.
4. Letter/fax – where one has an e-mail with much delayed feedback.

Most people like face-to-face communication. They believe it is more natural. It is easier to understand and be understood. That is, it better for picking up subtle cues about lying, nervousness or superficial rather than actual agreement. Business people also prefer to meet in groups in creative, decision making or negotiating groups.

Yet the scientific data suggest one-to-one meetings are more valuable. We know it is as easy to detect lying over the phone as face-to-face encounters. We know group brainstorming produces fewer good ideas than people working alone. We know group decisions are often more risky than individual decisions.

The rather stultified video-conferring makes the business of face-to-face communication more difficult. But it can record interactions which is useful.

The e-mail has considerable advantages especially for non-native speakers. It is cheap, quick with very fast feedback, and provides a record of the conversation. It allows the non-native speaker to formulate his/her thoughts and if necessary to check with a colleague. Sure it's a cool medium, but there is nothing wrong with a cool head in business.

Most business people feel that a good mix of media provides a better way of knowing and being known. Start with e-mails and then do a videoconference. Make a few calls and understand the importance of the distinction between real business and niceties. The more you use the new media, the more familiar and comfortable you feel. And the more often you are able to sleep in your own bed, maintain a private life, and monitor to control the in-tray and office politics. This is surely a good exchange for a handful of less and less desirable air miles.

Confucius was wrong: Remembering what you see, hear, read

It is attributed to Confucius that he said, 'I hear, I forget; I see, I remember; I do, I understand'. Alas he was only half right: often you remember very little of what you see – particularly on television.

Consider the following test: a homogeneous group of 60 people are divided randomly into three groups of 20 people. One group *watches* a 10 minute television news programme (that they have not seen before); one group *listens* to the same programme; the third group is given 10 minutes to *read* it. They are all getting the same information but through quite different media: audio-visual, audio-only and print.

After this they receive a memory test. The question is who remembers most and why? Ask any group to vote on what they think will result and you get the following: 70% believe the TV group should remember most; about 20% say it is the print group; and 10% (those pretty dedicated Radio 4 listeners) believe the radio group should have better recall. Asked to explain their choice, those who believe in the particular memorability of television talk about the 'impact' of pictures, the 'power of images' and so on. With few exceptions, the results of over 20 serious studies have been exactly the same: the print group remembers the most, the audio-visual least and the audio-only group in between.

If you ask very detailed and specific questions, you find the television group remember about a fifth of the details, the radio group about a quarter and the print group about a third.

People are often shocked about how little they can remember. But the question remains: why do the audio-visual group do so badly? There are various reasons for this. First, there is the issue of what psychologists call 'cognitive processing'. What they mean is intellectual effort. We have all come in after a 'bad day at the office' and slumped, malt-in-hand, in front of the box. It does not matter much what is on: it often washes past us. The next day nothing much is retained save perhaps a quirky remark or bizarre image. It's easier watching the box than reading the paper – it takes less effort. And it is this effort in reading that leads to better retention and understanding.

Television is pre-packaged. The 'story-line' is often extremely simple. Compare and contrast the content of all dreaded party-political broadcasts with the serious party manifesto. They are, of course, equally tedious except to the few – but the messages, images and metaphors in the broadcasts are aimed, it seems, at the hard-of-thinking. Write down the words that go with TV ads. It may be little more than a few clauses. They work on repetition – like radio ads – rather than understanding. Some try humour; others paradox. But the 'too-clever-by-half' ads often mean that one simply does not even know what the product is. So memorising and understanding takes concentration and effort.

A second reason for poorer recall of audio-visual material is synchronisation between the words and the pictures. Imagine being on a television news team. A disaster happens: the film crew is dispatched. They do their best to send pictures down the wire that 'tell the story'. But news keeps coming in. Those in charge of the script try to distil and précis the most important aspects of the story. But also they have to take some cognisance of the limited and dated pictures available. They rarely match: the story is complex with statistics; the pictures may be poignant. But the one does not necessarily reinforce the other. Like those badly dubbed foreign films of old: the mouth stops before the words are out. The word/picture discrepancy can be very off-putting – and it does not help concentration.

A third problem is speed: people read at different speeds as a function of all sorts of things including education, mother tongue, practice. Television comes at a pace one might or might not comprehend. Reading is self-paced; practice is also usually self-paced. This helps comprehension. Many people will say when re-watching movies how much more they picked up the second time. They also say that of novels but much less often. You learn best at your own pace.

The way material is broken-down and laid-out is important. Magazine and newspaper editors are careful about where in a page they put a picture.

Mind-mapping enthusiasts are equally insistent that memory and understanding is about links, connections and relationships. The chunking of the literature is important. Television has only one option and that is order. You can't put a news item on top of, next to, or below: only before and after. Serial order is certainly very important. We know that, under different circumstances, there are both primary and recency effects, meaning that either the information that comes first, or last, has most impact. We also know that (nearly) always the stuff in the middle is the most forgotten.

For the print medium, we have two-dimensional space: also, colour, word size, and cartoons can be used to break up text; to emphasise things. All you have on the radio is loud/soft, accents, speed and order. Television can change colour but does so rarely.

Research has shown unequivocally – a rare word in the social sciences – that people remember less of what they see than of what they hear. It shows without a doubt that reading is best – which is a form of doing.

Certainly there are those who learn best by trial and error. Surprisingly few computer manuals are ever opened. After all, you learn to drive a car not by watching others or reading books but by sitting in the driver's seat. The combination of a good instructor and opportunities to explore, fiddle and question leads to fastest learning.

So the ancient Chinese guru was part right. From what we know today we could say: 'I see, I forget; I read, I remember; I do, I can repeat'.

Creativity – and how to measure it

It seems to be an unstated, but widely held, assumption that all businesses need creative people. Some assume that creativity is both necessary and sufficient for business success. Creativity, whatever it may be, is clearly a very desirable characteristic and worth developing a reputation about.

The way people most often use the words 'to be creative' is both different from, and certainly more desirable than, being innovative. Innovation is about doing things radically differently. It seems implicitly assumed that creativity is special, innovativeness ordinary; that creativity is a rare gift; innovativeness can be learnt.

It is certainly true that one of the pathways to success in organisations is indeed through innovation. Some have rejoiced in the innovative product route. Disney, Polaroid, Sony and Microsoft typify this route to success. Others have developed innovative technology like Benetton, Honda and Evergreen. Some have tried to be innovative in the way in which they have a relationship with their customers. Some of the airlines (Virgin) and credit card companies have been successful doing this.

But other organisations have been extremely successful without any particular innovation. Some have simply explored the rigidity of their competitors like Federal Express or Easyjet. Others have turned around a slowly declining business like the Hilton Hotels. Saatchi and Saatchi arguably were successful not because of amazing creativity but rather by capitalising, mobilising and manipulating market forces. Some airlines have found success through the exceptional service route.

But still the received wisdom is that we all need highly creative people. And the search is on to find, recruit, manage and retain them. But is the gain worth the pain? If you can find them, can you effectively manage them?

Curiously, empirical research into creativity remains something of a backwater. Essentially there have been four rather different approaches: those who study the creative process; those who are fascinated by the creative person; still others who are interested in the creative product; and more recently those interested in the creative situation. The problem for the social scientist is finding an agreed real world criteria for creativity, so that the issue can be properly investigated.

It may be based on product criteria (patents awarded, number and type of publications), or professional recognition criteria, or social recognition, all of which are open to fashion, political correctness and the like.

There is both good and bad news when looking at the scattered scientific literature on creativity. The first is that it is true that both ‘creatives’ and psychotic mental patients share the ability to produce more unusual associations between words and ideas compared to that long but undistinguished group called normals. In the jargon, this means creatives and certain mad people have common information processing patterns which could be seen as deficits.

They seem unable to inhibit irrelevant information from entering consciousness. They find, whether they like it or not, unrelated ideas become interconnected – and this is often bizarrely a very creative process. They also both have high resting levels of activation and tend to be oversensitive to stimuli. Hence they may demand a special environment in which they can feel comfortable.

The extant research on creativity and madness suggests persons genetically related to psychotics are often unusually and statistically improbably creative. Creative persons often suffer bouts of serious breakdown and psychopathology. And psychotics and creative achievers have strikingly similar ways of thinking.

But of course madness is neither necessary nor sufficient for creativity. Most mad people (psychotics) are far from creative. And many highly creative people are more prone to neurosis rather than psychosis. Certainly, many creative writers have been prone to depression; but few (with some notable exceptions) have ever been hospitalised.

A recent study comparing equivalent groups of creative and non-creative 'normal' people brought to light the problems with managing creatives. The creatives were marginally more extroverted but much less conscientious. They were all less efficient, dependable, organised, responsible and thorough. In short they were lazy and self-indulgent – but they were creative by all accounts.

However the creatives certainly were artistic, curious and imaginative. They were marked for their unconventionality, introspective and unusual thought processes. But they were also distinctly neurotic. They tended to be self-pitying with brittle ego defences; they tended to be tense and prone to depression. People noted they were anxious and touchy. They certainly are impulsive and moody. Many seem overly concerned with their levels of adequacy. It maybe that neurosis is associated with creativity in 'normal' populations and psychosis in abnormal populations. Certainly if one has been around talented 'arty-fartys' for any time, it is not difficult to notice rather high levels of neurosis. But once again it must be emphasised that not all neurotics are creative – one does need raw talent.

Now you know why advertising agencies have account managers. These are relatively normal people who intercede between the client and the creative. Put the latter two together and you may expect sparks and a quick end to the business.

Don't be fooled at the interview. The creative person is not the marginally flamboyant figure in coloured bow tie dressed a little like George Melley. The charming person with a steady history both personal and professional is unlikely to be the real creative. Real creatives are likely to be pierced and have tattoos in places you never thought possible. Further, their daily intake of legal and illegal substances would also probably make you shiver.

By definition, the real creatives are difficult to manage. They are cold, manipulative and uncaring and they do not easily work in teams. Frequently absent, they often let you down. But some are clearly worth the investment and pain – but which. All however are difficult. After all, they score on both neuroticism and psychoticism. How do you manage the anti-social, ego centric and unreliable? The answer is with difficulty. But if you really care about creativity you may have to.

Culture change and how to manage it

The concept of change in business usually causes a mixture of anxiety and boredom: the former because change often hurts (is costly, time-consuming and frequently unsuccessful) and boring because so much is said and written about it. But considering changes to corporate culture adds yet another bemused negative reaction: puzzlement.

What is corporate culture? Can we define, observe, and measure it? Is it important to worry about or just another out-of-date management fad? And if it exists can it be easily or ever changed?

Anyone who has changed their job certainly recognises the existence of the unspoken (and often unspeakable) norms and values of the work-place – from how people dress and interact with each other to more important things like attitudes to absenteeism, time-keeping, team-work and customers.

Consultants like to talk about corporate culture because it is so obvious to them. Just walk into the reception of a company's HQ and you get the feel of the culture. Spend half a day talking to people, eating in the canteen, looking at the HR department's struggles and you have a pretty good grasp on the corporate culture – which, it is argued, is reflected in the all-important bottom-line data.

Academics from many disciplines have tried to offer definitions from the ever-inclusive and technical to the mundane: 'the way we do things around here'. Others have tried to categorise corporate cultures – nearly always into four categories associated with power achievement, task and process/role.

Perhaps the most interesting work occurs when consultants are called in to assess the culture of two organisations that are about to go through a serious merger and acquisitions. In one celebrated study of two American banks, it seemed as if they could not be more opposite. In bank A, the CEO's style was participative, egalitarian, externally orientated and he was called

'Buddha'. In the other bank, the CEO was authoritarian, elitist, internally orientated and called 'Dennis the Menace'. Bank A planned ahead, was people-orientated and had high community spirit. In Bank B it was 'Management by Crisis', task orientated and with low community involvement.

The banks had different heroes, different myths and different ideas of where 'paradise' was. In Bank A the hero was the first woman bank manager and the feisty VP of human resources. In Bank B it was the prior CEO and the treasurer. In Bank A, paradise/Mecca was to be in the branches; in Bank B it was the CEO's office.

The different cultures were even physically different. In Bank A, the eating facility was a plush, restaurant-like affair; in Bank B it was the spartan cafeteria lookalike. The branches for Bank A had the 'spare no expense' feel; but for Bank B it was all about 'avoiding embellishment'. Even the CEOs' offices were differently located: for Bank A it faced outward; for Bank B inward. It not take a genius to predict the M&A would be unhappy – especially for the people of Bank A. Indeed, it failed. (See also the *Digestif* at page 200.)

But if the culture is both a cause and consequence of both input (management style, work patterns) and output (profit, share value), it must be very important. And it may need to be changed when it is inappropriate to the business or even dysfunctional.

Classically, organisations try different strategies to change their culture. Some try more than one at the same time or in different orders depending on various factors like who is in charge; how successful the strategy has appeared to be; indeed the corporate culture itself.

The classic seven are:

The fellowship strategy

The fellowship strategy relies heavily on interpersonal relations, using seminars, dinners and events to announce and discuss what needs to be changed and how. People at all levels are listened to, supposedly treated equally, and conflicting opinions are expressed. This 'warm and fuzzy' approach emphasises personal commitment over ideas; but, the process may have serious problems getting under way, if at all. Because this strategy is averse to conflict, it can miss crucial issues and waste time. It rarely succeeds in changing culture.

The political strategy

The power structure is targeting by attempting to influence the official and unofficial leaders: the 'keepers of the culture'. The strategy seeks to identify and persuade those most respected and who have large constituencies and who therefore shape the culture. Political strategists flatter, bargain and compromise to achieve their ends, which is usually the introduction of new methods that reflect different values. But this de-stabilises the organisation because of continuing shifts in people's political stances. Maintaining credibility can be difficult because the strategy is so obviously devious and paradoxically often is the very opposite of the values that the new company is proposing in the new culture.

The economic strategy

This cynical culture change strategy believes that money is the best persuader. The person who controls the purse strings can buy or change anything. Everyone has a price. A serious increase or decrease in money will change behaviour which reflects the values of the new culture if sufficiently incentivised. This is the approach that assumes people act more or less logically, but that their logic is based on entirely economic motives. But 'buying people off' can be costly and the effects short term. The strategy also ignores emotional issues and all questions besides bottom-line profit. It too often is a strategy at odds with the new desirable cultural values of the organisation.

The academic strategy

The academic strategy assumes that if you present people with enough information and the correct facts, they will accept the need to change and how to do it. The academic strategist commissions studies and reports from employees, experts and consultants. Although such strategists are happy to share their findings, it is difficult to mobilise energy and resources after the analysis phase. 'Analysis paralysis' often results because the study phase lasts too long and the results and recommendations are often out of date when they are published. Also, most managers do not really know what they should do, to whom, how or when. And they often feel left out and ignored by the consultant academic.

The engineering strategy

This technocratic approach assumes that, if the physical nature of a job is changed, enough people will be forced to change. The strong emphasis on the structural aspects of jobs: what people do; and how and why they do it and what the realistic alternatives are. A major channel of communication can prompt structural change, but fails to commit most people. It is the method of re-engineering. Such change can also break up happy and efficient teams. The strategy is limited because only high-level managers can really understand it, it is impersonal and it ignores the question: 'What is in it for me?' But it can work well once those who can't change leave or get out placed.

The military strategy

The military strategy is reliant on brute force. The emphasis in on learning to use the weapons for fighting the law, the union, the media. Physical strength and agility are required and following the plan is rewarded. But the change-enforcer cannot relax, in case the imposed change disappears. Furthermore, force is met by force and the result is ever-escalating violence. It only ever works when organisations are in real crisis and seriously struggling to survive.

The confrontational strategy

This strategy believes that, if you can arouse and then mobilise anger in people to confront the problem, they will change. Much depends on the strategists' ability to argue the points, as well as being able to stir up emotions without promoting violence – and control them. This approach encourages people to confront problems they would prefer not to address, but tends to focus too much on the problem and not on the solution. Anger and conflict tend to polarise people and can cause a backlash.

Cultures change strategists divide on a number of issues: should you attempt to change the attitudes, beliefs and values or more simply the work-related behaviours of people? Should you use carrot and stick (reward and punishment) or just one or the other for most effect? Should one start the change process at the top or the bottom in organisations? Should one 'engineer a crisis' to really get people to come on board.

Certainly the literature and case studies give some answers to these dilemmas. It is probably quicker and easier to change actual behaviour than beliefs, so target what people do rather than what they think. Carrots work better than sticks – always. Young people are often easier or and more happy to change: so start at the bottom. And never engineer a crisis. That will backfire – Oh yes – real culture change is slow, different and requires living, not just talking, a new work style with all the consistent values and behaviours to match it.

D

Deselecting a boss

The business of selection, at least in theory, is very straightforward. One is trying to select the good (competent, motivated, talented) and reject the bad (incompetent, lazy, talentless). The two errors are therefore to reject the good and accept the bad.

One never knows when the first error has been made; with the second, one certainly knows and suffers the consequences. Someone selected that feckless, capricious, narcissistic marketing manager; no-one spotted that the engineering director was unstable, paranoid and passive-aggressive; and the selectors failed to spot that the quality controller was obsessional and compulsive; the head accountant uncommunicative, indifferent to others' needs and quite unconcerned about personal impression.

The reason for these errors is that selection appears to be concentrated on the select in, not the select out process. Selectors often have a list of ill-defined, inter-related and bland 'competencies' and appear to spend most of their effort looking for the evidence of them.

And interviewers commit a well-known series of sins sometimes called cognitive biases. Thus interviewers seek information about candidates consistent with their first impressions rather than information that could refute those impressions. Further, in forming those impressions, people underweigh that information which does not yield a consistent profile. Often the information that comes earlier is treated more highly than that which comes later. And certainly evidence of negative behaviours (be they sins of commission or omission) hold much greater sway than positive information.

The problem is that a selection interview is a charade; a hall of mirrors; a test of impression management on both sides rather than information search and evaluation. Both sides are on their best behaviour attempting to put their best face forward.

One of the most serious faults that leads to disaster is the belief that there is a linear, rather than a curvilinear relationship between a human characteristic and success. For instance, take intelligence: is it the case of the brighter you are, the better you do (the linear hypothesis)? Or possibly that one needs enough intellect and, once that point has been reached, increased intelligence has no beneficial effect? Or, and this is the curvilinear hypothesis, that intelligence is beneficial up to an optimal point but increased intelligence after that leads to poorer performance. The phenomenon is known in schools – the brighter children who misbehave through boredom.

And so it is with so many *positive* characteristics. Confidence is very desirable in all managers but the over-confident can be demanding, opinionated and as unwilling to admit mistakes as to learn from them. Conscientiousness too is desirable but this can spill over into zealous, critical, stubborn obsessional behaviour. Co-operation and compliance may at extremes lead to dependence.

Excitable enthusiasm may mask neuroticism and fun-loving mischievousness may easily conceal anti-social traits.

The moral of the story is that one can, quite simply, have too much of a good thing.

People have also a range of *negative qualities* that both have no desirable characteristics and which they take great pains to hide. What are they and how can they be detected?

Two are important and recognised but selectors are either embarrassed or feel unable to assess them. They are (again) intelligence and neuroticism. People need to be bright and stable enough to do jobs that involve skill: the pilot, the surgeon, the IT consultant all need to be bright enough to learn the skills (and how to update them) and stable enough to cope with stress. Many HR managers are uncomfortable around IQ tests and nervous of, as well as ignorant of, how to measure neuroticism. The latter is serious bad news as it is the harbinger of absenteeism, depression, anxiety, low morale, psychological disorders and so on. The former is supposedly measured by education, but that is insufficiently sensitive as a measure.

Another way is to provide a checklist of negative characteristics and attempt to ascertain a person's level or standing on them. A list of 20 is provided below to rate. Consider which are most important to *select out* and rank order them.

Read down the list and put a 1 next to the characteristic you think most undesirable. Then go onto the next until you get to 20.

		Rank
Biased	(Unobjective, inconsistent, unforgiving, favouritist)	____
Cowardly	(Pusillanimous, weak, unconfrontational)	____
Dependent	(Not self-reliant or confident or self-sufficient)	____
Devious	(Deceitful, indirect, lacking in forthrightness)	____
Dim	(Neither thoughtful nor logical, unintellectual)	____
Directionless	(No sense off direction or 'vision' or foresight)	____
Dishonest	(Lacking in integrity, untrustworthy)	____
Disloyal	(Perfidious, disobedient, disrespectful, whistle blower)	____
Fickle	(Capricious, lacking in perseverance and steadfastness)	____
Incompetent	(Slapdash, unproductive, both ineffective and inefficient)	____
Immature	(Foolish, inexperienced, lacking in wisdom)	____
Impulsive	(No self-discipline or self-control)	____
Narrow-minded	(Inflexible, unreceptive)	____
Selfish	(Unappreciative, unconcerned, insensitive)	____
Uncooperative	(Unfriendly, unavailable, unresponsive)	____
Unimaginative	(Prosaic, lacking in curiosity and creativity)	____
Uninspiring	(Depressing, dispiriting, unenthusiastic and not uplifting)	____
Unreliable	(Neither dependable nor responsible)	____
Unsupportive	(Oppositional, unhelpful, showing no understanding)	____

This list is actually a set of antonyms taken from a study where employees were asked to rank order the characteristics they most admired and wanted in their leaders and managers. The ones that came top were honest, competent, forward-looking, inspiring and intelligent.

If the opposite applies, the rank-order of the least desirable characteristics should be dishonest, incompetent, directionless, uninspiring and dim.

Studies of this sort have shown that three groups of factors seem important above all others: morality, competence and social skills or, if you prefer, ethics, IQ and EQ in that order. Beware immoral or amoral employees. There will be many temptations over the years and they need a sound moral base that both their bosses and reports will have to rely on.

Morality is associated with fair mindedness (not bias): with honesty (not dishonesty); with loyalty (not disloyalty) and with straight-forwardness (not deceitfulness). That for many employees, is what they seek most zealously in their boss, but somehow it never appears to make it to the selection interview.

They will also need to be bright enough to learn new skills as jobs change. From their intelligence often comes confidence, flexibility, imagination and courage. And they need a good dose of people-people EQ skills: this influences whether they are caring, mature, self-controlled and supportive.

Can you teach morality, intelligence and social skills? Certainly not intelligence, and EQ with some difficulty. Better to spend money on selection than training. And better to be equally concerned with 'select out' than 'select in' factors. Remember that dim, inadequate, immoral colleague of yours who got through the firms selection procedure.

Delivering a motivational talk

There is a new breed of animal stalking the country: the motivational speaker. Who are these people and what do they do? Who employs them and why? Is there any evidence of their ability to inspire others longer than the length of the seminar?

In one sense, there is nothing new about the concept of a motivational speaker. Our parents had Billy Graham, Lord Soper and, of course,

Churchill. Such speakers were nearly always found in religious or military contexts. They had the ability to uplift the heart; to perk up the dispirited; to energise the weary and to convert the indecisive.

Motivational speakers can make all the difference. But do they need to be heard more than once? Or will one wonderful talk do? And what qualifications do they need to be believed?

Ask average managers what they most want to know about and the answer is invariably how to motivate their staff. Some believe in sticks but not carrots. And some take a rather simplistic view, believing that money is the most powerful weapon to motivate people at work.

But weary managers who have been through the mill of managing a wide variety of people know that motivation is somewhat more complicated. They know that different things (money, titles, time off, physical environment) motivate different people. They also come to realise that different things also de-motivate them.

But all will tell you the story of the employees who are hard, if not impossible, nuts to crack. Their managers try every trick in the book. They buy books on motivation, hire consultants, go out of their way to find the spark in this group, but to no avail.

The second related problem is a sudden, often unpredictable, company/section-wide drop in morale. A down-turn in the market, a merger, acquisition or a history of poor management may lead to a quick drop in morale. A previously motivated workforce seems to lose its way. Lethargy, complacency and negativism abound.

So what's the answer? Employ a motivational speaker? Imagine if the hype and promise was true: you expose the unmotivatable or the temporality dispirited to an hour, even a day, of motivational speaking with the result that there is an immediate attitudinal and behavioural change. It is the stuff of managerial dreams.

Does it work? Maybe, though we have only anecdotal evidence. More importantly, how do motivational speakers actually perform? There are versions of the genre: the manic evangelist; the sincere Baptist; the serious comic. They are curiously very different in style but similar in content.

The manic evangelist is really an American export. They require lots of audience participation. One is required to jump, clap, scream, sing and perform other crypto-cheer leader activities in the course of the day. The sincere Baptist is the street corner preacher who tells his moving tale with timing, passion and anecdote. The serious comic is a night club act that is full of riotous humour but interspersed with the serious message – which may be delivered in a quite different tone.

Despite dramatic differences in style, the content of the motivational talk is remarkably similar to the sermon of old. To 'deconstruct' (as they now say in literary circles) the motivational talk is an interesting challenge. There are similar metaphors and techniques in all such talks. There is a lot of 'I believe' talk and repetition. Phrases that somehow 'taste good' are often repeated, e.g. 'Talent is not enough'.

But most of all, one notices the metaphors in the story. The first is the journey or often, the race. This emphasises both the past and the future. It is about having goals and the journey to reaching them.

The stories are also, of necessity, about fortitude, tenacity and endurance in the face of setback. What is inspiring is how the obstacle was overcome; how the failure turned into success; how the lesson to overcome the disappointment was the key factor. It's the solution to the problem of evil in theology: evil is there to teach us a lesson.

Another theme is the fall of the proud: how cockiness and egotism lead to failure. There is a lot of talk about the best/worst experience of one's life and how one learnt life's lessons that enabled one later to be a success.

Parents and friends appear in the talk. This is the social support/teamwork bit that managers like their staff to hear. So there is reference to synergy, interdependence and the necessity of give and take in teams.

The talk is deeply anti-fatalist in the sense that we make our destiny. We make our beds and we lie in them. We are, and can be, captains of our fate and master of our ship.

And at the heart of everything is the C-word uttered so often in business settings: CHANGE.

The theme is how, if you change your goals, change your strategy, change your life style, change your foolish ways, you too can win an Olympic gold medal, become the top salesman, or whatever.

Life is not a dress rehearsal. Unlike Marks and Spencer, you can't get a refund. With only the talent you have, enthusiasm, determination and a good team, you can WIN BIG.

Get the pace and timing right, tickle the heart strings with stories of joy and sadness and have a happy ending – and you too could be a motivational speaker.

But does motivational speaking work in the sense that it changes anything? Usually, delegates are invited afterwards to try to translate the main points of the talk for 'themselves at work'. They find this difficult either because the lessons are so bland and obvious, or else they know it really is different at work. It's different because they don't set or often identify with their goals. It's different because the game is not worth the candle. It's different because they really do not, and cannot, have control over their destiny.

People like (most) motivational talks. They are interesting and often uplifting. But the experience is a mood changer, rather than a belief or behaviour changer. Motivational speakers themselves will admit that it was well-timed and honest impromptu remarks that hit home and changed their lives, rather than set-piece motivational talks.

You change beliefs by changing behaviour – not the other way around. And you change behaviour by an astute and subtle mixture of carrot and stick. The secret is finding out which size and flavour of carrot and what diameter of stick has more effect.

Dress-up Friday

Let's face it: the dress-down Friday gimmick didn't work. Workers often did not like it. Customers were confused. Shareholders saw few benefits. Another daft idea was a predictable and predicted failure.

The reason many workers – dare one say women in particular – did not like it was because it only added another difficulty to the issue of how to dress. One needed a second business wardrobe – the 'smart-casual' look that was expensive and problematic. Smart-casual, like business-ethics and military-intelligence is an obvious oxymoron. Men, too, happy just to don the uniform, had to find something that was accepted and also expressed your 'individuality'.

Dress in all organisations follows a spoken, or rather an unspoken code. Dress code is part of the corporate culture and something you pick up soon after joining an organisation. Certain things are de rigeur and some taboo. It was said you had to be very rich, very senior (or very stupid) to wear a brown suit and shoes in the city - .except perhaps on Friday.

We have all had the embarrassment of arriving at a party over- or under-dressed. It is embarrassing because we signal our expectations about formality, measured by guests, food, wine. And being under-dressed insults the hosts; being over-dressed insults your intelligence. Both mean you read the invitation wrong – you made a social gaffe.

The theory of dress-down Friday is the theory of 'Dress makes the man' not 'you can't make a silk purse out a sow's ear'. The idea is that your clothes not only reflect your attitude but influence them. People are more comfortable in comfortable clothes. Dressing down, in theory, lowers stress, blurs false barriers between 'Chiefs and Indians' and promotes general wellbeing. But does casual dress lead to casual attitudes and behaviour towards customers, time-keeping and following company rules?

Psychologists have long wrestled with the questions of the relationship between attitudes and behaviour and particularly how to change behaviour. It's not unlike the old debate between productivity and satisfaction. The question is about causality: does job satisfaction lead to productivity, or are productive workers happier. The attitude-behaviour debate is much the same: do attitudes reflect or cause behaviour?

Assuming you want to change some form of work-related behaviour – obeying safety requirements, handling customer complaints, filing company reports in the standard format – what to do? Is it best to hold meetings, send memos and preach the gospel of what you want? That is, should you target attitudes and beliefs in the hope that logically the required behaviour will follow? Or should you 'change the rules' and by a mixture of reward and punishment ensure people do what is required. In other words, target the behaviour and let the attitudes fall into line.

What legislators find is that only some groups respond to attitudinal campaigns: the majority need legislation. Take seat belts: there were extensive 'clunk-click' campaigns but well under 50% of the population were regular belt users. So legislation was passed and it became illegal not to wear one. And whereas people used to 'belt up' to prevent being fined now they belt up because they believe the accident statistics. Attitudes in this sense follow behaviour – they did not lead to the behaviour.

If you want to change behaviour, target behaviour. If you want to change attitudes, target behaviour. And target it directly. The dress-down Friday (DDF) brigade was trying to do much by a far too crude and insensitive method. Some claimed the effect of DDF was to increase morale, others that it increased productivity, some that it reduced stress. No one seemed exactly to know what DDF was meant to do. Staff got either contradictory or no message about the purpose of the exercise. Some embraced it enthusiastically; others had to be told to dress up a bit. Clients had to be warned about the process.

The behaviour was targeted but the wrong behaviour. Formality of dress at work is a function of occupation and corporate culture. For electricians, builders and carpenters, every day is DDF. It would be both dangerous and preposterous for the uniformed services to have a DDF.

As an alternative to DDF, which is widely regarded as not effective and in fact leads to problems, some smallish workgroups hold an 'attitude readjust seminar' (ARS) on Fridays around 5pm (1645-1800). The name of the 'event' differs from company to company and time to time.

It amounts to a few bottles of wine, a packet or two of crisps or crudités. There is no set purpose or agenda save reward for the week's work, to review progress, to let off steam. Attendance is voluntary and participants may leave at any time.

Groups that hold these meetings say they fulfil an important function. Things can be said, especially upward feedback from juniors to seniors; a bit of bonding can take place; and where appropriate a little thanks given where it is due. Some groups hold their ARS every week; others fortnightly and still others once a month. But the fact that they tend to continue means they are probably found to be useful.

Perhaps, if you are after a bit of a booster to work group morale, abandon DDF and have an ARS instead.

E

Executive education and business performance

The executive education industry likes us to believe that learning pays. But this is just like marketers assuming advertising works in that it ultimately increases sales above the cost of the advertising itself. The problem is that there is precious little evidence to substantiate the belief that sponsoring an employee on an MBA or similar programme will even recoup costs let alone significantly, even noticeably, improve the bottom-line.

There is evidence that having got an MBA, one's salary increases. This can therefore be seen as a good investment for self-financing, middle-aged, middle managers who want to break through the next level of management. But what is the employer or the selector getting in your average MBA graduate? Additional knowledge and skills; guarantee of a particular personality profile; or merely reputation of being 'a shaker and mover'?

There is no doubt that executive education increases knowledge and, to some extent, skills. Whether they are relevant or quickly decline after the course has ended is uncertain. Graduates know a lot more about how business works and tend to have an impressively increased vocabulary – sort of 'business babble'. They may also acquire or enhance particular analytic skills – some of which are more useful than others. Sitting exams, and writing reports may have limited usefulness back in the work place but the case-study method can teach people how to appraise complex scenarios analytically. It can, of course, also lead to analysis paralysis.

But an MBA does not effect ability or motivation. At some institutions, but possibly the minority these days, getting an MBA is an indicator of ability because acceptance on a course is conditional on good, rigorous, well-normed ability tests. But the growth of business schools and the decline in applicants mean many have 'relaxed' their entrance requirements. An MBA is no guarantee either of ability or necessary relevant skills and knowledge to the business.

Is an MBA an indicator of personality? Certainly MBA students and those who self-select to go on programmes tend to be ambitious, need-for-achievement types. They have to be hard-working, well-organised, dedicated, self-starters. Less charitable people would say they are characterised by avariciousness, egocentrism and short-termism.

Or does the MBA act little more as a reputational placebo, the expensive sugar pill of management. Both the degree holder and those working with him or her believe in their ability, skills, judgement and effect on the bottom line which miraculously actually causes the latter to happen. However, it is more likely to be the beliefs and expectations of customers and shareholders that influence business performance, than deluded, star-struck or business-school-bamboozled certificate holders and their fellow travellers.

Business school students are notoriously demanding. They are more characterised by pragmatic exam-orientation than academic curiosity. They are hot on their rights; cool in their responsibilities. They play to their strengths rather than attempt to compensate for their weaknesses. Their education-work-life (im)balance means they have little time for those most academic of activities like wide reading, reflection, recreational debate – the essence of an academic education.

Could you prove the proposition that education really improves performance? Could it be done through the use of techniques used to determine the efficacy of drugs like randomised, double-blind, control trials? Certainly that methodology does have a lot to say about how to demonstrate real results.

To do this, one would have to do the following. Managers of similar age, stage, ability and experience from different parts of a big organisation would have to be selected for the trial. They would have to be as 'equivalent' as possible. Most importantly, they should be in sections where their ability, effort and style can be directly related to both objective (revenue, costs, absenteeism, productivity) and subjective measures (ratings of satisfaction, management style, climate). The more measures the better as any one is possibly unreliable.

The managers should be randomly assigned to one of two or three groups: one group does business education; another moral philosophy and a third yoga over the full duration. No-one is to be informed to which group they were assigned (done randomly) and the secret is kept on their return. This is a randomised, single-blind, controlled study. Then, after 6 months and perhaps again twelve months later you measure the business performance of the manager's section, group or department. If the business education group is significantly more successful in explicit, definable and measurable terms (try dosh) this is proof it works.

We know from psychotherapy research on efficiency that, oddly, all therapies have roughly similar effects. It could be the same for education. Studying Aristotelian ethics may be no more or less beneficial than accounting – because it is the educational process rather than the content that is important.

The various forms of psychotherapy do share some important features, as do all types of education.

- Psychotherapists all rely on the therapeutic alliance – a relationship between therapist and client that is characterised by acceptance, caring, respect and attention. This relationship provides social support that helps clients deal with their problems and acquire social skills that they can apply to other relationships. Presumably, the longer and deeper the acquaintance, the more powerful the effect on the client. The same is true of teacher-pupil; professor-professional MBA student. Education of all sorts improves self confidence.

- In nearly all forms of therapy, clients talk about their beliefs and emotions, how they act, and why they act that way. They examine aspects of themselves that they ordinarily take for granted; in so doing, they gain self-understanding. Just explaining through talk – even to a tape recorder – may therefore have beneficial results. Again the same is true in seminars, whatever the topic.

- The mere fact of entering therapy (education), whatever the method, usually improves the client's morale. The therapist conveys the message ' you are going to get better': the teacher 'you are going to get more insightful'. Clients begin to think of themselves as people who can cope with their problems and overcome them. Just expecting improvement can lead to improvement, although not of course if expectations are unrealistically high. The business school message is no different. You will become richer, more competent, more perspicacious.

- Most important, perhaps, every form of therapy requires clients to commit themselves to making some sort of change in their lifestyle. Simply by coming to the therapy session, they are reaffirming their commitment to attempt to overcome their problems. They are also obliged to work on that change between sessions so that they can come to the next session and report progress. Improvement often depends as much on what clients do between sessions as on what happens in the sessions themselves. And this is the essence of adult education. Giving up free time to studying anything is a big commitment. It is a behavioural commitment to do things differently.

But at this point nervous business school deans and marketeers start raising objections: we are all team workers and business performance is a team effort (not up to one manager); in some parts of the organisation (i.e. HR), performance is not really measurable and so on. That is flim-flam. Ask them about performance management, selection and promotion decisions, and whether those are informed by data. Of course performance is difficult to measure – but it is not impossible. It takes time care and effort. What exists, exists in some quantity and can, in principle, be measured. The truth is, like the snake-oil salesman, they are fearful of the results of the trial.

Humble trainers, as opposed to sexy consultants, have long been asked to justify their budget by proving that training works. People measure training by four methods.

1. The first is **participant reaction** to training. Measures of trainee satisfaction through post-course 'happy sheets' is cheap, easy and relatively straightforward. But it is important to make sure the evaluator, and not the teachers, choose the questions you would like the course participants to answer. Trainers can easily bias the questions to their known strengths. Entertainers get excellent feedback but teach little. Getting students to evaluate their MBA is dissonance reduction or buyer's nostalgia. Most rationalise the idea that it was worth it, irrespective of what they really learnt. This is therefore not a good measure.

2. Second, there is **learning**, which is the difference between pre- and post-course knowledge and skills. Again, this is not too difficult to measure, although there are two important caveats. It is easy to make the pre-test very difficult and the post-test very easy so that it looks as if the trainee

has learnt a great deal. Also learning, unless practised and reinforced rather than punished, is all-too-soon forgotten. A 360° feedback assessment pre- and post executive training can provide a good indicator of this.

3. Third, there is **behavioural change**, which is what the trainees do differently. This can take months to measure, and for most involves considerable effort. It too may be best judged or rated by others – preferably by subordinates of the trainees/course attendees. It focuses on differences. This is an excellent way to measure performance but change itself does not necessarily mean improvement in section/department results.
4. Fourth, there are the elusive results from the **bottom line**. All sorts of things can be measured – sales or productivity up; rejects, absenteeism or customer complaints down. Training and education is not only about this of course. It could be seen as a developmental opportunity that enhances employee satisfaction rather than company profit. That is a perfectly acceptable goal but organisations must be honest about it.

If an individual's contribution to business performance cannot be measured, all human resource decisions must be based on guesswork. One only has to see small business – a pub, a bakery, a corner shop - 'change hands' to know what difference an individual manager can make.

Business schools need to invest in a study that proves business executive education really does improve performance if they want to make that claim.

Expectations and how to manage them

What is it like to work for BA or the BBC? What do they look for in their potential employees and how do some make it to the top in these organisations? Once you get a job, what are your promotional prospects?

One could argue that one of the most important functions of managers is to manage the expectations of staff. They probably do this best on a one-to-one basis in progress reviews or appraisals.

Managers need to act very much like doctors. They have first to explore the beliefs of their 'clients' (i.e. employees) to understand their ambitions and hopes. Once they have found out what the beliefs and wishes of their reports actually are for themselves in the workplace, they can begin to challenge, change or correct these beliefs – if erroneous.

But because managers avoid appraisal, it is quite common, particularly among new recruits, to have very biased views about their career in the organisation. Some of these expectations can be dealt with at, or just after, the selection interview. Managers have to make explicit that which is implicit. They often need to answer questions certain people want to know the answers to but are too afraid to ask.

Consider the dozen questions below:

- What percentage of people interviewed are offered jobs?
- How many people don't pass at the probationary hurdle?
- What is the typical period of time before successful new people are promoted?
- What does the average middle manager in this company earn?
- Typically, how long do people stay with this company?
- How does the company deal with those going absent (unauthorised), caught pilfering, or having an office affair?
- What is the company policy on supporting you (with time or money) doing an MBA?
- Does the company favour promotion from within or getting new blood from the outside?
- Does the company (still) offer you a (real) career?
- Is loyalty rewarded or punished?
- How important is the annual appraisal for decisions about promotion and performance related pay?
- The company talks a great deal about getting the home/work balance right: is it serious?

Nearly everybody would be interested in these questions. It is of course possible most managers (even the senior ones) don't know the answers themselves – which means they too may have odd expectations based on ignorance. One of the most interesting theories in 'motivational' psychology is expectancy valence theory. Put simply, it goes like this.

First, do you believe that if you put in extra effort, time, and concentration, it will result in higher work performance? That is, to what extent do you believe you alone are able to control your work outcomes? Clearly, if you believe it is due to others, machinery/ technology, fate, supervisor moods etc. you are unlikely to be motivated to put in the effort in the first place.

Next, to what extent do you believe your better results (from the harder effort) will be noticed, recorded or rewarded? If they are not logged and related to some sort of reward, why bother? It is surprising how many jobs have no regular, sophisticated and sensitive way to measure output.

Third, supposing extra effort leads to higher output which is rewarded. What is the value of those rewards? Is the game worth the candle? Rewards have different valence at different periods over the life cycle: younger people are more sensitive to money; older people to time. Some will do anything for a job title – others don't care a fig about what is written on their card.

The theory says the three components are multiplicative. That means if any one is zero, the whole lot is zero: there can be no motivation. So motivation is about three forms of expectancy: self-efficacy expectations, boss-sensitive expectation and reward-salient expectations. Three hurdles on which to fall!

And, therefore, employee expectations need to be explored. Further, they can be changed – in both directions. That is, you can turn a healthy instrumentalist into a fatalist by removing control from him or her. Equally, through showing people that their ability and effort do make a noticeable difference, the fatalist can be taught to become an instrumentalist. But it takes effort.

Managing expectations is a very important task for all managers. It is particularly important when people join organisations that their hopes and aspirations are dealt with realistically. Ignoring this issue only stirs up problems for the future.

Exit interviews

Some companies worry about high staff turnover; others clearly wish they had more. Organisations like fast-food restaurants and insurance companies learn to live with extensive staff turnover as a matter of course.

But when an organisation begins to feel that it is losing its best people, haemorrhaging its talent, or simply experiencing a sudden loss from particular departments or sections, questions have to be asked.

Most managers have their own theories as to why staff leave. These range from poor pay (which helps to explain why they can't take the pressure) to a poor selection decision in the first place (no doubt made by someone else) or else the particular person refusing to fit in/adapt to the particular corporate climate.

But others are not so sure and try a bit of research. This usually involves little more than the increasingly popular interview given to those who voluntarily quit rather than those who are compulsorily fired or laid off. The theory is that such interviews can fulfil simultaneously a number of functions. They supposedly help an organisation modify causes of attrition and other festering corporate problems. They may help job-leavers by giving them a chance to ventilate anger or disappointment and lessen these emotions because the employer is seen to listen and care. In this sense, the exit interview is more about damage control and prevention. Psychologists call it catharsis.

At the most mundane level, exit interviews are about 'leaving protocol' including the orderly and sensible recovery of employer property (passes, badges) and ensuring that buildings and accounts remain secure.

How do they work? The exit interviewer is usually chosen from the HR function deliberately so as not to have been the 'exitee's' line manager. Ideally, they are benevolent, avuncular, 'good listeners' who take the departing employee's side. They are trained to be like clinicians and counsellors: non-judgmental, focused entirely on the employee and his or her experience. They have a set of standard open-ended questions, the very last of which is 'what are the main motives for you leaving?' They are trained to ask questions like:

- How did you feel you were managed during your time with us?
- In general, how do you feel this organisation is run?
- What could have persuaded you to stay with us another five years?
- Looking back, what are the worst decisions you/your boss/the management made?
- What did you enjoy most/least about your time with us?
- Who/what will you miss most/least in the organisation?
- How would you rate the work climate/corporate culture?
- What did you think about your performance and salary reviews?
- What are the fundamental things we need to change to avoid loosing other good employees like you?

What is interesting about these questions is that they should all have been asked earlier – probably by the boss at progress review. The fact that no one asked the questions (save the last) is no doubt a partial indicator of why the person chose to leave in the first place!

Interviewers should expect the unexpected emotional outburst: rage, tears, shouting. They should take rough notes, including whether they would rehire the person if they applied; or, more poignantly, what lessons there are to be learnt for hiring others in the future.

Part of their agenda is to understand the exitees' view of their compensation and benefits package and to influence it where appropriate.

The factors influencing departure are well known. They are both push and pull factors: unhappiness at the place of work combined with the attraction of other jobs (grass being greener). Factors cited include quality of supervision; relations with co-workers and subordinates; work load; job security; flexibility of working hours; salary and benefits; location/commuting distance; personal family matters.

From the employer's point of view, the idea of the exit interview is eminently sensible. In fact, it benefits the employer most. It can gather useful information, soothe psychological wounds and prevent people turning into whistle-blowers and terrorists, subverting the organisation's reputation after they have left.

But from the point of view of the job-leaver, it has few benefits. It is tempting when faced by a sympathetic senior person in the organisation, to unload one's frustration and fury built up over the years. The data-dump of emotions may feel cathartic but is probably ill-advised. It is unwise to burn you bridges if you are in a small world – small town, small sector, senior levels. What goes around comes around. Remember the organisation takes notes on what you say at the exit interview. It still goes in your file.

The best pieces of advice are two-fold: dissimulate or remain shtum.

You should not say, even if true, that your boss was a dim, irascible, egocentric psychopath. The line to take is that he or she was competent and professional but that you two had a 'personality clash' - an excellent 'catch-all' but meaningless term to cover all disagreements. Don't say your work was humdrum, stressful or tedious – talk of moving on to new challenges to upgrade your portfolio and extend your horizons. Don't bad-mouth your colleagues, even if they were backstabbing, unsupportive weirdos. Say (persuasively) that you will miss the companionship and helpfulness of your work group and the friendly atmosphere you experienced.

Be warm and regretful or act like a prisoner of war giving name, rank and serial number …and that's all. Hand over the keys and bric-a-brac and leave. Never apologise and never explain. And, do not sign anything. They may want you to sign the interviewers' notes or some other prepared statement by the HR function. If pressed to sign a document, say something about sending it to your lawyer for a quick verification. Chances are you won't hear a thing ever again.

Paranoia may be healthy. HR practitioners are told that a good exit interview may help limit costly legal action and other bad publicity by a disgruntled employee. Remember the notes of the exit interviewer could always be Exhibit A in some file somewhere.

One of the main problems of the interview is timing. People in the grieving business talk of a wet and dry ceremony. The burial/cremation is full of shock and tears; the gathering to celebrate someone's life held six months later is altogether more measured; more balanced.

The emotional stress of leaving (even in the most happy of circumstances) can lead to inaccurate, unreliable exchanges from both parties. Resentment overcomes reason, emotion overcomes evaluation. The grief process takes time and people can reflect more accurately on what they miss, have lost and feel. Thus it may be best to have an exit interview 6-9 months after the person has left. They may be invited out to or back to lunch to discuss, on reflection, the issues the company wants to know about.

The advice for the existing employee remains the same – but from the company point of view, it means they may gather some really useful intelligence from the delayed exit interview if they know what they are doing.

F

Flexible workforces

A new buzz-word in the Human Resources World is the 'flexible worker'. The organisation of the future, we are told, is neatly divided between core and contingent workers. The former are few in number and nearly all 'wunderkinder': MBA-certified, multi-lingual, computer whizz-kids who are simultaneously leaders and team-players, with global vision but who understand local markets, who maximise profit ethically.

Contingent workers on the other hand have one high advantage: that is they are flexible – at least from the company's perspective. They may be part-timers, short contractors, interim managers, home-based teleworkers or outsourced suppliers. They may be relatively senior and experts in their area or they may be what organisations call 'casuals' - and that is as much a reflection of their dress and attitude as their contractual arrangements.

Companies see the advantages of these contingent workers. They are probably easier to hire and fire. Those who work from home don't have all the expensive overheads. Students, foreigners and others who are flexible may be less litigious and less aware of their rights and stifling work-place regulation. Many are the minimal wage earner with minimal job satisfaction and minimal motivation.

Years ago, British Rail introduced 'flexible rostering' for drivers. It caused a strike – and it's not difficult to see why. Train drivers of the time were essentially shift workers. And what shift workers often like are the opportunities for non-work activities like childcare and pursuing various hobbies. They, like everyone else, prefer routines. In that sense, the term 'flexitime' is a misnomer. Morning people start and finish early by choice while those with different body clocks do the opposite. And they are not flexible in the sense that early-birds and night-owls stay that way. It is, we think, biologically hard-wired.

What the flexible rostering debate was about was the fact that it was good for BR if the drivers could be posted their duties at the last moment or were able to be switched should the occasion arise. It meant fewer cancelled trains and if it worked in the long run, possibly fewer drivers. They were flexible. But consider the position from the driver's perspective. He or she could never plan ahead, accept invitations or have a stable pattern of work. Being flexible to BR meant being at the beck-and-call of the needs of the railway. A sort of butler to the travelling public. From the flexible worker's perspective, flexibility has a rather different and definitely negative ring. Flexible means vulnerable; it means casual; it means easily expendable; it means second class.

It is not so much fun being a flexible worker, still less a teleworker. People on anti-social shifts or working from home can feel very isolated. They do not identify with the organisation – or feel very valued by them. They can feel used (and abused) and reciprocate the lack of trust.

A flexible work contract can lead to a pretty uncommitted 'psychological contract'. Just as adolescents often have short, stormy, ineffectual and volatile relationships, so do flexible workers with their organisations. If you feel your company does not really care about or value you, it is pretty easy to reciprocate the sentiment.

High status flexible workers like inter-managers and out-sourced experts do fare better. Some, like the early retired, prefer the short-termness of flexible working. And some of them have the power to make sure the company is flexible for them. Indeed that is the nub: flexibility often means others accommodating to your needs.

If core wunderkids are so marvellous, why are they not flexible too? Indeed, one sees in many companies, particularly those in the financial sector, a very interesting set of contradictory messages. At the same time, they say sagely and sadly that the 'career is dead': no-one should expect lifeline employment in any one company. We are all portfolio, short-term, contract, mobile workers now. But on the other hand they are desperate to find and keep their star wunderkids. They get golden 'hullos', golden handshakes, and flexible golden packages. They are knowledge workers and thought to be absolutely crucial to the company. 'Keep them at all cost' seems to be the message. And then we are the flexible company: one who is prepared to adapt to the individual – and their extravagant demands.

Hypocrisy or clever strategy? One could decline various human characteristics thus: I am firm, he is stubborn, they are bloody-minded. It may be possible to do the same with flexible: I am flexible, he is inconsistent, they are unpredictable.

Fitting the right person to the job

Thirty years ago, when life seemed so much simpler, the job of HR consultants, managers and researchers could very easily be described in the epithet: 'fitting the person to the job, and the job to the person'. Now we have recruitment, assessment and selection specialists for the former and operation and development and ergonomic specialists for the latter.

Yet it remains crucial that HR specialists can ensure an adequate supply of the right people, at the right time, for the available specified jobs. Whether one prefers to see employees as an asset or a cost they can be measured along various criteria like replacement value (how much it would cost to replace and train them to current levels); market value (the going rate for equivalent employees); maintenance value (through training, job enrichment); transfer value (the profit involved in attracting/transferring particular individuals); and output value (literally the measurement of work output).

Even non-HR people know the rudiments of recruitment and selection. First there is some sort of job analysis (observation, interview, task analysis), looking at the abilities, skills and ideal traits of the optimal incumbent. Then a look at the sources of supply: internal, education system, labour market, consultants and head-hunters. Advertise, interview, assess: trying to match what is known about the job with the applicant's knowledge, skill, experience and personality.

Is it easier fitting the person to the job or the job to the person? Consider the problems involved in fitting the person to the job. This is the world of vocational guidance and selection. The idea may be pretty simple: you assess both (person and job), hopefully in the same terminology and along the same dimensions, and look for fit or misfit: essentially a lack of disparity.

In fact, there is only one good theory in the whole vocational psychology that does really define people and jobs in the same terminology. It is Holland's theory and he has a hexagonal model with six types: realistic, enterprising, artistic, social, investigative and conventional.

But the problem lies in the concept of change. Jobs change -faster than ever. Certain jobs disappear – the linotype operator, the telegram operator – others change out of all recognition. Technology shapes the job – though of course we can sometimes adapt the technology to our needs. Technology usually means fewer people with different skills. Sometimes, skilled crafts people are reduced to being computer monitors: other times, they have to significantly upgrade their knowledge and skill to survive the way the new job is done.

But selectors make three consistent errors: they select for a particular job; not a series of jobs; they do a current job analysis rather than a future job analysis; and they rarely try to understand a person's capacity for change.

Starting with the last issue first, because it is perhaps the most difficult; do people change much over time? If so, what changes and how much? Physique, abilities, personality, beliefs, values? Those who believe in change should perhaps attend a school reunion or look at the data where people have been assessed as many as 50 years apart. People have remarkable capacity not to change. For instance, studies both of quadriplegics and lottery winners show their levels of happiness two to three years after the dramatic change in their lives resort pretty much to pre-trauma levels.

Sure we get older: greyer, wider, balder, wrinklier, even slightly shorter. The energy of youth is lost – but outward-going, sociable extroverts hardly change into introverts. Political opinions do change: who was it that said if one is not a socialist at 20, one has no heart; if one is a socialist at 40, one has no head? People with a taste for ideology can replace one 'ism' with its opposite. Marxism, as that old scoundrel Muggerige found, could quite easily be replaced with Catholicism. But social beliefs in the young are shaped as much by personal insecurity and peer pressure than reason.

For someone of 25-30 years, what you see is what you get. If they are good with numbers, have low EQ, are pretty conscientious and have no musical ability, there is unlikely to be much change when they are 60. Certainly, they may be less quick tumbling numbers; they may have learnt a few tricks to compensate for their low EQ; they may be less conscientious because they have been badly and inequitably managed; and they will probably still be tone deaf.

People's capacity for change is primarily a function of their intelligence and values. The former predicts ability to change, the latter willingness to. You need both.

The second problem lies in a future job analysis. Imagine you are selecting a pilot, or a teacher, or a call-centre operator, or a soldier. How different will the job be in 5 years? What skills are likely to be the same? Is any aptitude to do the job now, paradoxically, going to be a handicap for the acquisition of future skills? The problem is that the person has to be able to do the current job and the future job. Of course, it depends on how long you need the person for: the shorter the hire period, the more one can be 'now' oriented. But even five years can be a long time – and many changes can occur.

So selectors have to be something of a futurologist: they need to do a bit of serious thinking about how, when and why the job will change so that when they select people they can consider their ability at various points in time.

The third issue is related to the above. Most people do not stay in the same job for very long. The good ones get promoted to managerial roles where they no longer require the skills to do the original job but a very different skill set. The problem arises if people are extremely good at a job (often highly technical) and deserve reward which is mostly promotion. So we see all too often the brilliant sales person as a very unhappy and unsuccessful sales director; or, more commonly, the superb IT specialist quite unable to manage anybody. Some companies give managerial titles with no management responsibilities to cope with this problem, while others consider non-specialist managers: that is, the idea that IT managers or actuary managers are not IT or actuary-trained themselves.

Certainly, if one is in the 'High Flyer' world, the need is not only to select a person for a current job; but also the next job – and the job after that. This means considering attitude to, aptitude for and appetite for management. This is quit tricky in a 25-year-old specialist, but quite necessary.

Fitting the person to the job is as much about person analysis as job analysis. Too many consultants have an expensive and impressive armoury to do the former but a pretty empty 'tool box' for the latter. And it may be that the latter is now more important than ever.

G

Growth and development

When HR consultants and other psychobabblers say 'growth and development' they do so as if they are synonyms, but they hide an important distinction. A stockpile of products grows, but does not develop. To grow is to get bigger. Managers can develop without growing – they increase their skill, insight and ability to satisfy their own needs and the requirements of the company.

Development is concerned with the increase in capability and competence. Organisations, like countries, may grow and/or develop. Growth is about standard of living; development, about quality of life. One can reverse growth much faster than development. Indeed, the more developed are the individuals or organisations, the more judiciously they can use resources for future development.

Some organisations talk about growing managers, and have OD (organisational development) plans. Others have development workshops and centres aimed, one hopes, at skill and knowledge acquisitions. Most organisations talk a good line about 'growth and development' but see it somewhere between an HR fad and a bull-market luxury.

But others take it very seriously. Those into growing people at work are not unlike those dedicated to animal husbandry. They know they get the best out of their stock by giving them the best grazing land, the ideal water conditions and so on. They can be fattened for market, turned into a very productive dairy herd, or best kept in ideal conditions for use as artificial inseminators – by being grown to their potential.

The agricultural analogy is indeed a very good one for managers to think about, irrespective of whether one is growing livestock or grain. Choose the best seed; choose good land; water, weed, fertilise; rotate the fields; allow fallow periods – all have easy managerial analogies. The fallow period may be a sabbatical; the rotation a secondment to another company or part of the organisation.

There are essentially two models for growth. First, there is the Darwinian: Survival of the Fittest model. This suggests, at least with regard to management, that you choose the best people you can. Then you test them, in a wide variety of settings: job transitions; implementing change strategies; taking on more and more responsibility and being influential in non-authority relationships. Developmental opportunities are essentially about overcoming hardship. Job challenges reveal most talent because the best survive. Therefore the more challenges given to the person and the better he or she survives, the more likely they are to do well later.

The second model is agricultural: Grow the Best from the Best Husbandry. It also suggests that you select the best you can. But then the task is to consider how to nurture the plants/animals to get the best out of them. This means making sure the environment is best suited to this and to 'give them a hand' when they need it. It means planning for the best cycle and anticipating a development schedule for the different stages involved. The best comes from those whose potential is developed the most.

The idea of growth is to ensure that each person achieves his or her potential. The idea of development is that they exceed that potential. GM crops are about development, not growth. A GM seed is hardier, more fruit bearing, more pest-resilient than the ordinary seed that may be grown to fullness and harvested under ideal conditions.

In some senses, growing managers is much more passive than just developing a plan for each of them. But a plan is needed for what you are trying to achieve and where you are trying to get to.

There are probably six steps to growing a manager and three steps for developing them.

1. First, **select good stock** or seed (ability, personality, EQ, IQ). Ability, stability and motivation are a must.
2. **Prepare the land or environment** (equipment, office, corporate culture). Give them an ideal corporate climate to work in.
3. **Enrich the land** by weeding, watering and fertilising (update all

systems, deal with problem people). Don't rest on your laurels. Make sure issues don't fester; that people are trained and re-trained where necessary.

4. **Rotate the crops**: (encourage a variety of experiences). Use the Japanese method of secondments to different parts of the organisation or different subsidiaries in different places to enrich experience.
5. Occasionally **let a field fall fallow**: (give genuine 'time out' opportunities). Make sabbatical real: encourage, where possible, educational or travel opportunities during these periods.
6. **Understand the preferred plant/animal/personal/ environment** in which they thrive (look for the best fit of person and environment). The fit between the person and the job is dynamic. It requires re-adjusting, re-calculating and re-setting.

But developing a manager is something rather more than just growing one. There seem to be three fundamental steps.

1. Look for hybrids to go one step further: (seek out the unusual combination of talents). This is the inductive method of observation and trial and error.
2. Encourage non-affected and non-egocentric quirkiness. Allowing talented and creative people to work in their own way not only increases their satisfaction but also their natural way of being productive.
3. Through funding, be serious about continuous learning. This is a fine line between incentive and coercion by trying to make sure managers acquire and practice new and salient skills.

So what are the signs of success or at least that a person is worthy of growth investment? There are around a dozen: find six consistently and it is probably worth trying to develop that person.

- First, they seek out the opportunity to learn; Are they proactive, enjoy skill/knowledge acquisition? This is the first requirement.

- Next, morality: do they act with integrity? Are they honest and do they take responsibility for their actions? The latter is particularly noteworthy, very important and often neglected.

- Third, can they adapt to cultural differences? Do they actually enjoy and are they sensitive to cultural variation in business and social life? This is an index of ambiguity tolerance or how to deal with uncertainty.

- Fourth, are they genuinely committed to making a difference? Are they really willing to make personal sacrifices? Do they really want to have an impact on the business as a whole? Beware those who bluff and flimflam on this one. If they are only in it for short-term aggrandisement or gain, let them go!
- Next, they must seek broad business knowledge: they should be interested in the whole business. They must go beyond the area of their professional expertise. They must be interested in the big picture.
- Sixth, are there good reports that they bring out the best in people? Do they have talent to create effective teams, working environments? Do they understand individual differences and try to develop others?
- Seventh, and quite a hard one, are they insightful, even intuitive? Do they see things from new angles? Are they quick to see trends, and are they good at taking the perspective of the other?
- Eighth, are they courageous and willing to take risks? It is important that they are not afraid to go against the grain, will persevere in the face of opposition and can confront poor performers. Courage, as outdoor trainers say, often is one of the most important but one of the most neglected managerial traits.
- Ninth, do they proactively seek and use feedback? Is there enough evidence that they actively pursue, respond to, and use feedback to genuinely learn from others?
- Tenth, do they learn from their mistakes? Can they change direction when necessary, and start again after setbacks? Are they undefensive about negative feedback?
- Penultimately, are they open to criticism? Can they handle criticism well? Can they understand the difference between criticism of self vs. one's ideas?
- And lastly, have they got healthy coping strategies when under stress? Do they know how to seek help from the right people at the right time?

It's a long list but the time and cost in really developing people means you must be sure you have the right materials in the right place. Real managerial wunderkinder are hard to find.

Getting wiser

There are many different sources of information to suggest that (alas) other people don't change much over time. The first is everyday anecdotal information: go to a school reunion and see how little people have (really) changed. They are older, slower, greyer, wider and wrinklier – but still the same. Sure you may be wiser more perspicacious, more confident, but they don't seem to be. What is surprising and perhaps reassuring is that they have changed so little.

We also have lots of anecdotal information that is more frustrating: failed attempts to change others or even ourselves. Motivating the apparently unmotivatable; calming the neurotic, energising the lethargic and re-engaging the alienated. Intensive support, training, even therapy does not seem to help. They remain stubbornly the same, impervious to change. Remember poor Woody Allen? He's been to therapy for 30 years and is still not better. Changing habits, let alone personality is indeed phenomenally difficult.

And changing yourself can also be depressingly difficult. Try losing weight, giving up smoking, reducing drinking. It is equally difficult to start something like regular gym visits as well as stop them. We are creatures of habit. But are we slaves of our personality and genetic inheritance.

As well as everyday experience, there is now accumulating good evidence from longitudinal study that people do not change much over time. Both abilities and personality seem remarkably stable.

To give two examples: recently Scottish researchers have retested hundreds of octogenarians on the same IQ test that they did in the 1920s. The results showed correlation of .6 to .7 indicating bright kids grew up to be bright adults and bright oldies, while the dim essentially stayed that way. And of course intelligence had a massive effect on people's lives relating to the health, wealth, and welfare – even their longevity.

Other studies, this time from New Zealand, involved all the children born in the early 1970s, for over 30 years. They found that 'personality' characteristics manifest at three years predicted an incredible range of behaviours at age 26: alcoholism, attempted suicides, recidivism, partner beating, etc. And other personality test scores remained very stable, even though they had had very different life experiences.

Still stable after all these years? Sure but why. It's interesting to demonstrate – against the hopes of many counsellors, clinicians and trainers – that people don't change, but the really interesting question is why. The bride who thinks, 'I'll alter him' as well as 'aisle, alter, hymn' needs to know why her hopes are essentially unrealistic.

The answer to the question is essentially threefold, nicely summed up in three words – reactive, evocative and proactive process.

First, personality and ability dictate how people see the world differently. Go to a film, a play or a new city with someone and notice how they seem to perceive and experience the same thing quite differently. The paranoid see challenges, the neurotic threats, the narcissistic complements and the adventurous excitement. That is, people react to the identical situation differently as a function of their personality and ability. In this sense, it is impossible to give people the same experience – be it a training course or an appraisal. Your personality is a filter of reality: it determines how you react and therefore people can react to different situations similarly or vice versa depending on their personality.

Next, people tend to evoke different responses in others. Neurotics' moodiness tends to lead to very different responses in others than do stable individuals who are less prone to ups and downs. You only have to be in the presence of someone who is very good looking, very bright, or very extroverted, to notice how they evoke quite different responses compared to the average individual. Extroverts put people at their ease more than introverts.

Any parent knows that different children evoke in them very different emotions and parenting styles. Naughtiness evokes spanking; compliance evokes praise. How people respond to you is therefore relatively consistent because abilities and traits tend to lead to responses in similar ways.

The third process is productivity. People choose and change situations in accordance with their personality. Extroverts choose noisy situations, introverts quite ones. Consider how people arrange identical furniture in identical offices to reflect their personality. It can be arranged to signal dominance or optimise interaction. It can reflect artistic taste, which has also been shown to be part of personality.

Thus, through these three processes, we see and create situations to make our world stable. And this explains the paradoxical findings of geneticists, who study twins throughout their lives – time. Twins get more alike over time. Test them at 8, 28, 48 and 88 years of age and they get more alike in their attitudes, beliefs and behaviours. Most people would believe the opposite because, as they get inevitably exposed to different environments, they should change as a result of this differential experience.

But through the process of reaction, evocation and proaction, people seem to ensure their experience of the world is surprisingly tailored to their personality and ability. So they stay much the same.

This of course has very important implications for people at work. It means that, at selection, what you see is what you get – well, that depends on their impression management ability. School and university grades give a good indication of ability, which probably gets a ceiling in promotability.

Personality indicators can also be found in education and work history. Extroverts are sociable, out-going, sensation seekers. They seek out opportunities for social interaction, get bored easily and trade off speed for accuracy – and they always will. Neurotics tend to be hypochondriacal and prone to emotional outbursts and, perhaps more importantly, surges of conscientiousness are manifest throughout their careers. Primary school reports can predict behaviour in the prime of life. Some people 'go the extra mile', obey the deadlines, keep promises, refuse social loafing, pay their dues. They have the work ethic – indeed it is a personality variable and a predictive one at that.

People don't change much over time because their personality and ability ensures a continuity of experience in line with their character. And that is not very easy to change except in extreme situations – which explains why trauma rather than therapy leads to extreme change in individuals.

Guru babble

Crank 'science' books far outsell most books by reputable scientists. The same is true for management science. Yes, there is such a discipline and it is not an oxymoron. It attempts through experiment and observation to understand the process of management.

Yes, it's a young and immature science; true there are few robust findings and even fewer 'big theories' but it's a pretty difficult thing to research. There are lots of factors to take into consideration at the same time.

Paradoxically, the whole area is given a bad name more by its 'popularisers' than by its hard-science sceptics. Strictly speaking however, they are not popularisers or translators of science, but self-diagnosed gurus who propagate their own unresearched theories in the hope of making a pile of greenbacks.

There are many things you have to do to write a popular best seller or come up with a magic bullet solution to all intractable problems. The solutions must be simple, memorable, positive, and universal. They must be full of psychobabble, quasi-spiritual insights and crypto-capitalist philosophy. Managers must be seen as caring heroes. Managers have control: unions and economic forces are underplayed. Nothing must be counter-intuitive, but heard-it-all-before common sense needs to be disguised in psycho-organo-guru babble.

Simplicity: The book should have a simple message supported with plenty of memorable anecdotes, vignettes and stories.

Changeability: It should underscore the point that human behaviour is changeable despite the evidence – and that there are seven crucial skills to acquire.

The individual as the unit of analysis and change: The successful business book must be psychological in its focus on people and underplay organisational, economic and political factors that shape organisational success.

Managerial Control: It must stress the techniques that increase and improve a manager's control.

List of steps and principles: It should provide a road map to management or a simple guide to how to achieve success. This is the paint-by-numbers of the management world and there should be about seven steps.

Universality: It is important that the book suggests its ideas have universal application and appeal. None of this multicultural, diversity nonsense in a best seller – the idea is that the secret formula works everywhere for all groups and for all time.

Short-termism: The book must claim or demonstrate some short-term payoff or benefit ('quick win'). Curiously, it is short term but lasts forever.

Success Stories: Ideally the book should provide lists of Happy Customers and those who have successfully adopted the ideas. Anecdotal evidence is king. They are often the author's friends or clients.

Self-confirmation: The book must not be counter-intuitive. Self-confirming approaches endorsing prior ideas and beliefs are essential. That is why so many repackage common sense and the things people already know. But they must come up with catchy concepts like spiritual intelligence.

Unitary perspective: Boss and employee, management and union have ultimately shared goals and mutual benefits.

Mills and Boon School of Business: Finally, the book must stress the nature of business leadership as a romantic, heroic enterprise. This perhaps says it all – the more like a fairytale it is, the better readers like it.

So there you have it – the 11 features of successful business book writers. But, alas, it's not very memorable. The list is too long; it's not really catchy. There is no mnemonic. One essential task of the aspirant guru is to have a 'theory'. This may be a 'model', which is a few boxes connected by arrows; but more likely it's a list. It may be a list of dos and don'ts like the ten commandments or, more likely, it is a list of qualities one needs to find in a great leader.

People interested in research on leadership write lists. One researcher listed those found or suggested by writers. There were 25. The research in this tradition is inconsistent and non-replicable. The list of traits simply grows over time, leading to confusion, disputes and little insight into why leadership traits operate as they do. The trait approach identifies people in leadership roles after they have been seen as successful. It is not certain therefore whether these traits make the leader or whether the leadership role shapes the traits. The trait approach may also be thought of as a fundamental attribution error: that is, explaining the behaviour (success or failure) almost exclusively in terms of the internal traits and motives of leaders, while ignoring or underplaying organisational, social and economic factors that clearly play a large part.

For years, psychologists have talked about the 'magic' number 7 (plus or minus 2). It is the holding capacity of short-term memory. People seem to be able to recall and deal with between five and nine pieces of information quite well. Go much over ten and they forget and confuse the issue. Teachers, trainers and leaders have long known this.

It is for this reason there are nearly always 7 (plus or minus 2) essential wassanames for every successful thingamajig.

H

Holiday Stress

There you are sitting on a dazzling beach under a gently waving palm tree. The blue-green sea, dotted with just the odd luxury yacht, sparkles under the clear azure sky. There are handsome, well-heeled, half-naked people on the not-too-crowded beach. Smartly-dressed waiters who speak good English and are trustworthy, helpful and cheap, are on-hand to top up your exotic cocktail. The children play happily somewhere else under responsible supervision. Your partner is contentedly doing his or her own thing.

The plan is to finish your novel and have a quick dip before changing to enjoy the alfresco romantic dinner under the stars. Fresh lobster, Chilean chardonnay, tropical fruit dessert. You have found an exclusive but affordable destination without hassle and life is great.

But then you wake up. You are actually on a vastly over-crowded beach with over-weight, bolshy Europeans. There is a pervasive smell of chips, sun-cream and sweat. The natives are surly, resentful and intent on ripping you off. The hotel, which faces the evil-smelling and noisy power station, is small, dirty and has never heard of customer service.

The children are either bored or sick or both and a constant pain in the proverbial. They whinge constantly about being given more money and want to do dangerous sports, stay up all night and hang around with local hooligans. They seem embarrassed by you and want to disco all night and bake all day.

You don't want to go shopping again and have had another row with your partner. Once again you find yourself in an over-priced bar getting steadily pissed and pissed off. You have an angry partner, frustrated children, a hangover and an empty wallet. And it has just started to rain.

Holidays are meant to be fun. They are supposed to be about relaxation, recreation, repair – quality time in a different environment. The theory is that they represent the opposite of stressed, monotonous, over-pressurised and uncontrollable work. Cynics argue that holidays are a time off work to remind bolshy employees that their organisation can get along quite nicely without them.

But the opposite is too often true. Holiday companies and airlines report a steady increase in complaints and litigation. Some therapists report a surge in bookings directly after the holiday season. The autumn it seems is a good season for divorce. Why is it that holidays so often fall short of the ideal and become, instead, a source of stress?

At home, there are clear roles and rules, and personal and private space. Who does what and when and why tends to get fairly well established. Some of these are traditional sex roles but others refer to who makes the early morning tea, who makes the bed and so on. And we all establish rules about meal and bed time and alcohol consumption and allowances (pocket money and what it 'covers'). Most importantly, the house is carefully arranged into public and private space and the latter further divided into carefully marked territories. The study, the den, the sewing room, the play room but most importantly the teenager's bedroom, the parents' en-suite are all private places where one is secure, unobserved, unobservable.

But holidays throw all of these into confusion. The rules are relaxed and maybe openly flouted. There is, in psychobabble, a great deal of role ambiguity. Thus teenagers who speak the local language better than their parents may do the adult negotiations while the deposed patriarch looks hopelessly on. Most importantly, the whole family are often thrown together in a much more restricted space with little privacy. Everyone complains, no one is happy. No wonder confusion is one of the first things you feel on holiday.

1. Unrealised expectations

Holidays are like Christmas, in that everyone makes high emotional and financial investment and the fantasy of a perfect occasion is seldom met. Holidays are short, looked forward to, infrequent, expensive and precious. Small wonder then, that emotions ride high and fuses are short if the fantasy does not materialise. Like Christmas, holidays involve a lot of 'specialness' – things reserved for once or twice a year outings. New wardrobes are shopped for and outfits not worn until the holiday itself. Hats and luggage are stowed for most of the year, to be brought out for this special time. Guide books and maps may be purchased to be used in advance. The fantasy may begin months earlier with the brochure. Special documents (passports, visas) may need to be acquired, injections (a source of phobia to some) be borne. Holidays often represent months of saving and are a significant item in the annual family budget.

Just as at Christmas, all wives expect their husbands to behave with the perfect manners of an Andy Williams clone; in the same way holidays founder on the fantasy of reinvented personalities. On holiday, one pitfall is to expect to be accompanied by a suddenly transformed, perfect family. In the sunshine, so the fantasy goes, the children will cease to fight and bicker and the husband will suddenly have no desire to drink large quantities of beer and watch football. All swearing will cease and for two weeks of the year the family will make the Oxo family look incompatible.

The reality is much different. Children will, alas continue to read their books instead of admiring the expensively-bought scenery; adolescents will sleep in their rooms instead of exercising in the expensive sunshine. Bad habits do not disappear as the star rating of the hotel increases, nor does libido always rise with the air temperature, another source of unrealised expectations (too much or too little).

For many, holidays are for acting out fantasy – but fantasy may be, and probably is, different for all family members. Tension occurs if one or more people are dissatisfied; hence the need for communication of desires, needs to find best compromise for all. Father may feel eating out is best to give mother a break from cooking: she may be anxious about children's diet and behaviour in restaurants and prefer the control of self-catering. Everyone has their own 'script' for the perfect holiday, but the script needs to be shared with others in an assertive fashion – no-one can mind-read.

2. Clarifying Expectations

The first problem with the holiday occurs early in the planning phase. Family members fail to clarify their expectations or hopes for the holiday. Some want to play at being an anthropologist, others an ambassador. For some, chilling out in the sun, to be deeply oxymoronic, is enough, while for others it is an ideal opportunity for retail therapy in a different setting. Teenagers look forward to the night life and many a middle-aged mother has fantasised about a Shirley Valentine holiday.

The central question is: what do the various family members want and hope for? What is their ideal holiday? Have they ever experienced it, to check whether they really know the answer to the question? What are the key ingredients to make the time both relaxing and recreational? Try an evening discussion over dinner at the planning stage. And you may no doubt be surprised what you learn about your family.

This exercise will no doubt cause confusion and depression as the family will discover desperately disparate hopes for the holiday. But this is the right stage to do it – no point ignoring the issue. One solution is to agree a destination with multiple opportunities and then decide a rota for each person. That is, Monday is Mum's day – she chooses what we do; Sunday is son's day and so on. If the family wish to stay together for activities, then the best option may be to give everyone a few attempts at planning the schedule. It can be done before the holiday but fine tuned on it.

This may provide yet another opportunity for family members really to get to know one another. Indeed it seems like an ink-blot onto which they project all their fantasies. But the idea of taking turns to set the itinerary sets a model for sharing, turn-taking and being supportive.

3. Understanding of roles

Building a routine where everyone understands their roles, can significantly reduce holiday stress. A routine reduces uncertainty, a major source of stress and fatigue. Holiday routines can be applied to many different types of holiday. They may be developed consciously or unconsciously. Many apply to things such as: same person always responsible for carrying tickets and passports; same person always prepares car; plots route; packs suitcases; shops for drinks and provisions while away. Children can develop roles too, such as fetching water/buying bread on campsites; setting the table if self-catering. Roles different from those at home make the holiday more fun (different = special).

4. Routine

Children love routine and holiday stress can be reduced if it is made 'home from home': favourite toys/games/books; familiar blanket/ bedding/nightwear/travel cot; own bottles/dummies/plates/cutlery. If space if short, older children can be allowed to choose just one special thing to take. Smaller children should be over-ruled – one two-year old was adamant that teddy was not going to be taken on holiday, until bedtime on the first night away. Stick to meal and bedtime routines if possible.

5. Doing homework

A related point is to do one's homework about the destination. There are two extremes when choosing a holiday: an impulsive choice based on price, brochure, television programme or recommendation, which really is like buying a pig-in-a-poke. The other is the protracted obsessional research project through the dark winter months to provide the authentic, perfect, bargain.

What do you need to know? You need to know the typical weather, not the generalised optimistic flim-flam from the brochures. Johannesburg is freezing in mid-winter, the mosquitoes in Alaska in mid-summer are some of the worst in the world; Hong Kong is overcast from Christmas until Easter. You need to know the peak season and who else tends to go there. Cuba is refreshingly free of Americans; the Germans love Thailand. You need to know the currency and whether it might be advisable bringing in cash from elsewhere. The paradox in Cuba is that despite there being no Americans, every transaction is in dollars. Deutschmarks work well in Turkey and East Europe. And in Zimbabwe, paying in any hard currency is welcome.

It might not do you any harm swotting up on a few local language phrases before you go. And finding out the tipping policy may prevent at very least misunderstandings. A rudimentary understanding of the history of the country helps. You can get Marmite in Cyprus and Malta because they were our colonies, but don't be hopeful in Sardinia. Find out if it is worth taking duty free – indeed, your drinking habits may be somewhat different to the locals particularly in Islamic countries. Get a good guide book and read it. The world maybe shrinking but its still tough getting camera batteries in Cambodia and sun cream in parts of Slovakia. The cost and frustration of getting it wrong is worth the effort of doing research.

6. Packing

A related point is what you take. Again there are extreme reactions: the hippie approach argues a change of t-shirt, and a credit card is really all you need. Others take everything from (literally) their security blanket to three changes of formal wear lest they be invited to three cocktail parties on successive nights. But you need to think about electrical equipment and the need for adaptors; photographic equipment, medicines and, most of all, amusements. Boredom and ennui are lethal ingredients on holidays, particularly for adolescents.

So, as the trainers say, proper preparation prevents pretty poor performance. For many, the ingredients of holiday stress are there long before you get aboard the plane. But as we all know, the five hour delay at Gatwick at the beginning, plus eight hours trying to get off Kos often render the holiday as stressful as staying at home. Being confined to a crowded airport, patronised and starved of realistic accurate information about the flight is everyone's nightmare.

7. Journeying

As noted above, it is no accident that the words travel and travail are etymologically linked. Travel, at least the modern form of it, is just as likely to broaden the behind as it is the mind. Successful travel is as much about attitude as it is about following rigid codes of behaviour. It can be an enormously exciting, beneficial privilege, which one's friends rightly envy. But all too often, it results in confusion, exhaustion and little success. There are two ways to cope with long flights or other frustrations.

Withdrawal/avoidance: This technique involves taking your mind away from the immediate situation: immerse yourself in a book or newspaper, which you can really 'get into'; go to sleep; daydream or fantasise; make plans, lists, think about future projects at work or leisure; take tranquillisers; gain access to the quiet, other-worldly atmosphere of the airline lounges.

Distraction: By providing additional stimuli, the source of stress becomes less significant: shop at the airport/station. Not for nothing have shopping arcades sprung up at airport terminals; eat and drink; play games, watch TV; strike up conversation. Self-disclosure to a stranger can be very therapeutic; take disinhibitors (for example, alcohol).

Almost everyone finds the following useful for reducing travel stress: take an 'adult comfort blanket' along – anything from a favourite type of sweet to a hot water bottle; have your own amusements to hand – the crossword, a laptop, books; mark out your own space with coat/jacket/briefcase. Adopt defensive seating to create security – a corner, the end of a row.

New and unfamiliar airports are a joy to the extrovert seeking kicks, but yet another source of terror to the unstable introvert. There are many anxieties in store for the recently 'displaced' traveller. Getting through customs, dealing with the reception committee, finding the hotel, understanding the currency and working out the language are just some of the hurdles which await the traveller.

The stress business is big business. Surveys seem to be showing that everyone is stressed at work. Some are stressed because they are not at work (redundant, retired, a victim of restructuring) others because they are too often at work. One reads about marriage (as opposed to marital) stress and moving house stress; the stress of Christmas; of exams and even the stress of shopping. Things have come to a pretty pass when we think of holidays as stressful.

Culture Shock

Culture shock, like jet lag and nervous-breakdown, is a term often used but little understood, that holiday makers claim to experience. It has six components:

1. Strain due to having made various adaptations in terms of living accommodation, food language spoken etc.
2. A sense of loss regarding the familiar items - media, family, comfort foods.
3. Feelings of rejection - you despise the natives and they you.
4. Confusion in who you are and what you believe. Are you rich or poor? How do they treat their animals or servants, and what can you do about it?
5. Indignation and disgust about suddenly becoming aware about certain cultural differences with respect to food, gender, time-keeping.
6. Feelings of impotence such as not being able to understand the currency, the language and so on. No wonder culture shock is a horrible surprise. And be prepared to experience it the more you are attracted to one of those long-haul, exotic, as-yet-undiscovered destinations.

Destination Expectations

Stress occurs when expectations are not met. One family had the best holiday in years in a large resort complex in Tenerife. They arrived to find the stuff of nightmares: a cement mixer parked outside the window that was started with the rest of the building site at 7am. The 'double accommodation' for parents was two single beds nailed to the floor at right angles; the 'inclusive breakfast' was two bread rolls left in a plastic bag on the door handle. Yet, because they had booked this holiday last minute on a 'cheap and cheerful' basis, their expectations were actually exceeded and the drawbacks (which were not health or life threatening) became a source of humour.Yet the same family, if booked into a 5-star hotel, could have found a source of stress if the towels were not changed often enough or the pool area were crowded.

Journey Expectations

Car/plane journeys are tedious and boring for everyone. If you expect delays and plan accordingly, not only will you reduce the stress of finding yourself in a regional airport at 2am after a five-hour wait, you will be pleasantly surprised if your plane takes off on time and your expectations are exceeded. Pack accordingly, with more nappies/juice/milk/wipes/changes of clothes than you think you could possibly need. Adults and children alike find car travel physically restricting and tedious. Plan frequent stops but don't make the stops exciting - the children will not want to come back into the car. Time journeys to suit your families sleep programme, if possible, but don't be surprised if excitement over-rules the biological clock. One family sacrificed a night of their prepaid holiday to travel in the evening when their one-year old usually slept. With pyjamas and his usual bottle, they expected a quiet journey. In the event, he shouted for the entire car ride, falling asleep only as they turned into their road. One family has a detailed routine for checking into a hotel. After checking in, the wife views the room while the husband goes on a 'recce' of the resort. It is his experience that she seldom finds the first room offered acceptable, so he allows time for her to inspect a second or third offering and simply finds out where she is from reception later. He does not understand her criteria for an acceptable hotel room and prefers to find a local beer: she likes to find a suitable room and unpack without pressure from a thirsty husband.

Planning

- Do research.
- Be organised.
- Plan in advance.
- Allow time for delays on the way to the airport.
- Allow extra time for getting children ready.
- Leave as little as possible to the last minute.
- Double the money and halve the clothes.
- What children's things can be hired there rather than taken?

Safety

All parents are concerned about health and safety on holiday. It can be a major source of stress if the hotel turns out not to be child-safe. Check in advance things like status of room balcony (can large gaps be netted?) Find out how to child-proof a hotel room (the internet is a good source of information), things like taping down wires to the carpet with masking tape. Take a small first-aid kit and check medical insurance cover.

How to complain

The British, unlike the Americans, are poor complainers. Purchasing a holiday is like purchasing a product: you need to know what to do if it goes wrong or fails to work entirely. Lacking a known procedure in a foreign language can be enormously demanding of an individual and, with the emotional/financial investment involved, stressful. Further, it is usually one individual or family against a large hotel, airline or tour company and it is clear why complaining is dreaded by so many and frequently ducked in the British spirit of 'not wanting to make a fuss'.

If you have a problem on holiday following this simple four fold approach there-and-then may help the situation:

- First describe the issue. Narrate specifically and unemotionally the time, place and frequency of the action. Don't be vague or emotional and, initially, don't attribute motives. Let the person know what occurred.
- Next, express your feelings. State your feelings calmly, relating them to the goal you want achieved. If you express negative feelings to a person, do so only in terms of the offending behaviour, not their whole personality, their nationality or the company they work for. No passive-aggressive sulking or sarcasm.
- Then specify what you want. Request all the reasonable changes, one at a time. Specify the concrete actions you want stopped and those you want to see performed. Take account of whether the person/organisation you are addressing can do this without major significant loss of time, money of 'face'. And say what behaviour you are willing to change to make the arrangement. Don't start mentioning lawyers, the press and so on at this stage.
- Finally, make the consequences explicit. Tell them what will happen if you are not completely satisfied. Reward people for any attempts to change in the desired direction. Emphasise the positive consequences for all concerned.

Ten tips to reduce holiday stress

1. Clarify everybody's expectations and hopes and manage where appropriate.
2. Agree a turn-taking schedule if you want to do things together.
3. Do your homework to avoid unpleasant surprises. Find out something about the local language, weather, currency, attractions, health facilities.
4. Travel light, travel mid-week; bring amusements for delays.
5. Book for a minimum of two weeks and a maximum of four. The first is for 'winding down'; the last (of 4) may induce ennui and boredom. Three maybe ideal.
6. Pack preferred family amusements if you encounter weather or delay problems. And pack some medical backup.
7. Pace yourself in your drinking, partying, sun-exposure. Exercise moderately given your age, stage and level of fitness - no 18-30 nonsense!
8. If you have young children or teenagers, consider going with another family so that people in similar age groups have companions. But make sure you know them well, like them and share similar hopes, expectations and preferred ways of holidays.
9. Be generous with your time, money and support for others. Treat the opportunity as one of getting to know each other better.
10. Lighten-up. Life is not a dress rehearsal. Enjoy yourself in your personal way.

Having expensive conversations

Trauma victims have counselling, CEOs have coaching, young managers have mentoring and the disturbed have therapy. Most people 'sort-of' know what happens in counselling and therapy, though they maybe hard pressed to distinguish the two. But the average person is puzzled by the new rage for executive coaching.

What is executive coaching? Is it little more than an expensive conversation between a friend-starved CEO and an avaricious consultant? Is it really anything other than counselling for top managers paid for by the company? Do coaches provide an excellent, discrete sounding board for an isolated boss? Or do they lead to a curious and dangerous dependency where the manager is unable to make a decision without phoning the coach?

First, a few conceptual distinctions. Mentors come from the inside; coaches from outside the company. Frequently mentors are allotted to 'mentees' while people choose their own coaches. Mentors are sometimes, but not often paid; coaches always are.

Perhaps the best way to try to understand the function of the coach is to look at the different types available.

A – The therapist-counsellor

Look at the background of a number of coaches, particularly in America, and you see the tell-tale signs of therapy – both received and given. Of course, therapy and counselling are not quite the same. Therapy is problem-orientated, counselling is person-orientated; therapy focuses on both the past and the present and is interested in revolutionary change, while counselling focuses on the present only and tries evolutionary change. Therapists treat, interpret and intervene to develop new ways of solving problems and improve functioning. Counselling is about caring, enabling, facilitating, supporting, exploring, discovering (blah blah) to alleviate suffering, find solutions to problems and deal with crisis.

Psycho-coaches also come from various schools. The non-directive approach celebrates just that: they don't give advice but help you come to a solution. The Freudians rake up the mud at the bottom of the pool from childhood in the search for both an explanation of, and solution to, odd, paradoxical, and counter-productive actions in adulthood. The cognitive behaviour therapists aim to explore and change thinking patterns.

But do CEOs need therapists any more than middle managers or supervisors? Possibly – they probably have more pressure and stress. But aren't they selected (and certainly rewarded) for their robustness and steadiness under fire. Is this form of coach a necessity or a luxury? A prophylactic or an analgesic?

Certainly some CEOs need therapy, but rather than a liberator, it can be a jailor. Some top people have been in therapy for umpteen years and are still not better.

B – Confidant/Friend

It's lonely at the top. CEOs have to learn to be discrete with everyone, even the board. They may be privy to certain facts but certainly have the big picture. They know about the importance of morale, the nature of self-fulfilling prophecies resulting from self-defeating mind-set and the general malaise that can result from careless talk.

We all need social support from trusted friends. It's good to 'shoot the breeze' and to have feedback on our ideas. But who fulfils this task? The CEO's spouse can sometimes have this role, but not always. The CEO might know another boss in a different company in a different sector and the two of them can help each other with, of course, an unspoken pact of confidentiality.

But if a friend or spouse won't do, why not hire a coach? The role of this coach, then, is to be there: to be a sounding board, a shoulder to cry on; a non-judgemental support in good and bad times. They might understand the business, but paradoxically they may do better if they don't. The naive questions sometimes provoke the most useful thinking, particularly if they are about people or products.

The trouble with the friend model is that the relationship has no natural beginning or end. Moreover, the friend is paid to be a friend, which is an oxymoron. Confidant, confessor, sounding board, perhaps: friend no. Should sessions be regular or when the CEO needs it? How to select the coach and find the right chemistry? And, most importantly, how much should these people be paid?

C – The educator/tutor

There are many reasons why people float or meander to the top. Sheer ability and knowledge of the business are often complemented by an ego, ambition and temperament that may not be ideal.

No CEO can really pretend to have a grasp of all features of the business and they tend, in their management style, to reflect their professional socialisation and culture. The erstwhile accountants, engineers or marketing managers do things differently. They are sensitive to different indicators;

comfortable with different styles.

Wherever they come from, they need to 'keep up' with technical and legal changes, as well as keep an eye on global and local markets. To do so efficiently, some CEOs enjoy and benefit from conversations with business academics, writers and journalists. They have the time to study trends, to ponder processes and think through the issues of the time.

This model of coach is the instructor. The CEO expects wide knowledge. He or she has no time (or even inclination) to read the burgeoning supply of books and magazines dedicated to the business, but they expect the coach to do so and to provide a précis and critique. They sort of want a reversed Oxbridge tutorial where the tutor writes the essay instead of the pupil.

The educator may or may not be supportive and friendly. This is not the role. It is to update, to inform and yes (very directively), to advise. They come from academia often but not always and they are difficult to find – but probably worth it in the long run.

D. The wise judge

Wisdom is about broad enlightenment; the thoughtful application of learning, as well as insight intuition and good judgement. The word wisdom is bandied about in business, but quality is hard to find. Wisdom may or may not be related to EQ or IQ; intelligence or personality; gender or training.

Wisdom probably comes through personal experience throughout life from the inculcation of parental values to wide job experience. It is easier to recognise than to describe, which makes it a fairly dodgy concept.

Perhaps Charles Handy has it? Others might nominate Dickie Mountbatten, Gore Vidal, Alistair Cooke or Lionel Blue. Handy certainly sounds wise, though he may be a trifle over-extended and repetitive. The job of the wise judge is to listen, to reflect, and to offer advice. Every culture has its own version of wise men. The Beatles thought they could be found in India, while others are impressed by Christian mystics.

The wise judge 'does not do emotion'. They are not therapists or friends or tutors, though they may be a sort of mix of all three. Wisdom is not flighty or issue-specific. And it is very difficult to find.

The problem is negotiating a contract with a wise judge. Many require intrinsic, not extrinsic, rewards and they may easily express irritation with a dim, self-indulgent, psychopath posing as a CEO. Many are wise enough not to get involved in these sorts of commercial wisdom enterprises.

Whatever model you choose or have, coaching is expensive. It may be intellectually and emotionally taxing. It may eat up valuable time. But it is bound to be costly. The trick is to distinguish between a merely expensive conversation and a seriously good investment in improving CEO performance.

Integrity: Can you measure it?

We all know that (white) lying is prevalent and that we are not terribly good lie detectors. We have all been hoodwinked by sales people, potential employees – indeed hundreds of people, hundreds of times. Hence the interest in *integrity testing*.

Since the dawn of time, people have dreamed of measuring the 'Pinocchio-response', namely the observable physical reaction that always occurs when telling lies, but never at other times. Hence the excitement and enthusiasm for the now discredited lie detector or polygraph, which measured such things as heart rate, breathing, and sweating during questioning.

Alas, too many known innocents were judged guilty as well as a few guilty discharged as innocent. These are called false positives and false negatives. The problem is fairly simple: identical physical changes can result from very varied emotions including surprise, anger, fear, disgust, guilt or even serious amusement. The error is misinterpreting arousal as evidence of deceit.

The next hope for the lie detector was not physical but pharmacological: the truth drug (sodium amobarbital). The evidence of this 'breakthrough' alas shows that it does not increase the probability of honest responding. It does seem to increase recall but that is both accurate and inaccurate.

And so it is with various other ways of ensuring that people tell the truth or indeed can be detected when lying. The evidence for the following techniques is not good in that they are poor (and never fool-proof) at distinguishing honesty from lies: hypnosis, voice stress analysis, pupilometry (measuring eye changes), graphology and fidgetometers (chairs measuring movement).

So the lie detectors have investigated honesty tests: these may be administered by interview, pencil and paper or the web. They may consist of straightforward questions like, 'Have you ever stolen, liberated, or removed merchandise from your work place?' or 'Do you think others steal at work?'. Tests measure admissions of past wrongdoings and temptation to misbehave. They are non-punitive on wrongdoers. The trouble is that these tests often penalise particularly moral individuals. Critics argue that honesty tests measure many things unrelated to honesty: fearfulness, traditionalism, street-wiseness, admission of human frailty.

An obvious objection is that the tests are susceptible to faking. That is, people see through the test and consciously create a favourable impression. Possible? Well almost. Try the attached.

A Two Minute (Fakable) Integrity Test

This is a timed test. You have just 3 minutes to complete it. For each of the 10 questions circle either a or b, indicating what you genuinely believe or which has been true in the past.

1 a. I have never cheated on my 'expenses' in my whole life.
b. Most swinger orgies I attend have a minimum of 18 people present.

2 a. I am completely open and honest when giving performance appraisals.
b. For the right price, I would happily sell company secrets.

3 a. I fail to comprehend why people are so upset by child abuse.
b. I would happily reject an increase in salary to ensure the poorest workers were better paid.

4 a. I pride myself on my very impressive low absenteeism record.
b. Real fun is throwing Gideon Bibles into the hotel pool.

5 a. I buy all my own stationery: never have I 'liberated' pens, paper even paper clips from the office.
b. Most arguments are best solved by a good bit of old fashioned 'fisticuffs'.

6 a. I donate about a tenth of my post-tax income to charity.
b. Poor people remain that way only if they are too dim to steal.

7 a. I have never been late for work in my life.
b. Television grossly exaggerates how dangerous recreational drugs are.

8 a. Making private phone calls, sending personal faxes or emails on company time and equipment is wrong: I have never done it.
b. Cocaine improves both concentration and morale at work.

9 a. I have never stolen anything more valuable than a Lada.
b. All my responses on my tax form are completely true and accurate.

10 a. I would never lie on a personality test.
b. Toxic waste dumping in the third world is a viable way to reduce their debt.

J

Job analysis

The textbook approach to selection always stresses the importance of fitting the person to the job. Round pegs, round holes and all that. They emphasise that in recruitment and selection you begin with a good job analysis. Understand what skills, abilities and temperament is required to do the job and you have a blueprint for whom to select. (See page 80)

But do managers, even human resource specialists, know how to do a job analysis. It should be the foundation or building block of HR because everything (from appraisal to restructuring) should be based on the information derived from a job analysis (JA).

Several steps are involved in a JA. First, the activities, behaviours, duties and tasks of the specific job need to be fully described. Second, these need to be rank ordered for importance and frequency. Third, the critical abilities, skills and knowledge associated with each task must be identified.

A good job analysis goes much further than a job description or job specification. The former are wider, vaguer and shorter than a JA; while the latter is often based on a JA.

There are probably a dozen reasons to do, or uses for, a seriously good JA. These include:

- writing up an up-to-date and accurate job description
- being able to do an evidence-based job classification
- doing a proper job evaluation to determine appropriate pay levels
- informing job design restructuring which occurs quite frequently

- informing personnel requirements (aptitudes, attributes, knowledge, skills, traits)
- guiding performance appraisal techniques
- specifying training programmes to make them most relevant and hence effective
- understanding and guiding within company worker mobility to maximise fit
- ultimately improving efficiency and optimal work processes
- being aware of identifying and helping eliminating unsafe working conditions
- making human resource planning empirical and better informed
- fulfilling legal and quasi-legal requirements.

Inevitably, smaller companies spend less effort on JA than big ones who are pretty variable in how, indeed whether, they bother with JAs.

There are all sorts of methods of going about a JA, each with advantages and disadvantages. Those with an anthropological bent or who are simply voyeuristic, prefer observational methods. This may be a mix of the man-in-the-white-coat, sitting hidden in the cupboard with a periscope or stop-watch. Or it maybe passively shadowing a person, silently observing live or via video what is happening. Good observational studies yield a wealth of data without relying on dishonest or inaccurate descriptions of people on the job. But they can't get at 'mental acts' like thinking, and they tend to underestimate less frequent but potentially important actions.

A popular method is to interview job incumbents as well as supervisors, subordinates, clients or other knowledgeable sources. Multiple sources can help provide a comprehension, unbiased (or at least less biased) view of the job and what it takes. The disadvantages are all too apparent: interviewees may be unsightful or contradictory or, more likely, simply inaccurately distorting their answers because they are suspicious about the real motives of the JA in the first place.

Sometimes, job holders are asked to keep quite structured work activity diaries. They are supposed to show, over an extended time period, exactly what the job holder did: when, where, why, even how easy or involving each task was. Done well and honestly over long periods they certainly do give a detailed insight into job activities. But like questionnaires, they may easily be biased, and like observation methods, they give little insight into mental activities; even worse, the real reasons for the various activities.

For those of a psychometric bent there are many off-the-shelf questionnaires available. Probably the most well known is the Position Analysis Questionnaire (PAQ) which has nearly 200 questions. It measures six features of every job:

Information input: where and how people get information needed to do the job (visual, audio, input, etc.).

Mental processes: precisely what reasoning, planning, decision making and other thinking processes have regularly to be done.

Work output: what tools/equipment has to be mastered and what physical activities have to be performed to do the job properly.

Work relationships: what supervisory, negotiating etc. daily relationships have to be formed and maintained to do the job.

Work context: what are the typical stress, hazards and environments in which the job is performed.

Other characteristics: work schedules, salary bases, clothing required.

Like all questionnaires, they are quick and cheap, and can cope with mass testing. More importantly, they provide comparative, quantifiable data so that jobs can be compared across the whole organisation.

But like all questionnaires, they can have many disadvantages. Respondents may misinterpret questions or simply lie. Worse, they may refuse to take part or 'spoil' the questionnaire so providing much less useful data. Some of these questionnaires can be expensive to buy and some particularly if they require open-ended questions.

A fourth method is the critical incident approach, which some people favour because it appears to overcome many problems of other approaches. Job holders and others are asked to provide full behavioural descriptions of the most important 'critical' incidences or occurrences that they have to face. They are then asked to give examples of typical and exceptional, good and bad, desirable and non-desirable responses to each situation. These provide observable and measurable behaviours and give an insight into job expectations. However, the method is certainly time-consuming and susceptible to all the well known response biases like lying, memory distortions and so on. Also, the approach often spends less efforts at looking at mundane incidents and typical behaviour which must be the 'meat and veg' of daily behaviour.

There are also so-called 'objective' ways of doing job analyses. One can inspect records, training manuals, existing job descriptions or organisational charts. The trouble is that these records are often thin and outdated. Another method is the most interesting for the job analyst. Do the job themselves for a bit. Whilst this may be impossible, dangerous or simply daft for certain jobs (dentist, pilot) it certainly provides really useful data for jobs that can be easily learned. The analyst receives first-hand experience of all aspects of the job: mental requirements, social demands and emotional stresses.

Is all the effort of doing a JA worth the effort? Is the game worth the candle? Surely this is not really required in order to do efficient and effective selection, training and other functions.

There are three standard objections to JA. First, JA promotes individualism and ignores team-work. That is it focuses on the individual job and may unwillingly create old fashioned demarcation summed up in the old idea of 'It's not my job'. But this does not have to be the case. It is quite possible to do group/team job analyses

Second, it is argued that job analyses are too static, and too formal. That is, JA do not reveal the dynamic changes that happen in a job as it changes rapidly over time. In this sense JAs are out-of-date as soon as they are complete. They are also too formal, missing out on the vitally important job-related behaviours that effect mood, morale and intrinsic job satisfaction. It may be true that some jobs do change fairly rapidly, but not true that the majority do. Dynamic methods may be used to analyse dynamic jobs if they really are dynamic.

Finally some argue that, at least for senior positions, one is not selecting a person for a job but a range of jobs. That is, high flyers don't need job descriptions because the position they begin at will probably be radically different from the job they end up doing. This argument too is specious. How else to challenge a possible high flyer than see how they do at a particular job. If they have abilities and know-how above their station, well, all well and good and let them go. But if they can't hack it, they certainly don't qualify for the epithet of high flyer.

Job Analyses are, or should be, pretty fundamental to the whole Human Relations endeavour. It is difficult to see how any really thoughtful, let alone scientific selection, could be done without full appreciation of what a job incumbent needs to know, feel and do.

K

Knowledge workers

There are many ways to describe and categorise the social class of people. The crudest nineteenth century classification was based on how much you used your hands or your brain – or, of course, how much you inherited. Most people remember with affection that poignant 1960s skit of John Cleese, Ronnie Barker and Ronnie Corbett explaining the triparteid classification of class (upper, middle, lower) based primarily on their height and to a lesser extent their accent and dress. It was a stereotype but had that kernel of truth about it.

In the fifties, the Americans had a much simpler system – blue collar and white collar. The Registrar General's Classification system is well known at elections: remember the C2s (or is it Essex Man) who determined the fate of both governments. The full system is a sixfold classification: A, B, C1, C2, D, E, based on occupation. But in all theses systems, there are curious anomalies and it can very easily get out of date.

The British, it seems, remain uncomfortable talking about class. To foreigners the country is and has always been very sensitive about all the markers of class from the u and non-u language of Mitford, to all the niceties about social etiquette. There are innumerable markers of class, perhaps the most easily identifiable around food: what you eat, when, what you call meals and the nature of social intercourse during the meal.

Class, at least for most sociologists, epidemiologists and political scientists, is based on occupation. But occupations are changing. Some have disappeared completely: the printing compositor, the lino type operator.

Other have been created: webmasters for example. While others just get their little changes. Change, they say, is inevitable – except from vending machines.

Today we are back to the old three-fold classification. And now the classification is whether one is a Knowledge, Information or Data Worker. Knowledge workers are the new elite. They are the smart-cookies who command the biggest salaries. Knowledge workers create knowledge. They invent, adopt, merge information to create new products and processes. They are, of course, highly computer literate and numerate. They are masters of all new media and early adopters of all new technologies.

The difference between knowledge workers of this century, the upper class of the last and the aristocrats of the nineteenth century, is that in the past, the acquisition of skill and knowledge was slow and cumulative. Experience was a good thing. In the apprenticeship model, one acquired expertise over long periods of time and never lost it. Today, knowledge (and therefore skill) is more transitionary. This means there can be rapid mobility in class – both up and down. Unless one is clever with investing money made young and quickly, an older knowledge worker might find it really difficult to keep up with change; lose their cutting edge and sink down the social ladder and become an information worker.

An information worker may be both clever and skilled but is definitely in the second division. They know how to access, process and store information usually in a specific area but they do not *create* it in any meaningful sense. In this sense, they are reactive rather than productive. But they too have to 'keep up', particularly with technology. Their job is to store, classify and disambiguate knowledge. They are essential to the blue-sky knowledge workers much as a clever, well-organised PA is to a CEO. Clever ones see patterns and connections, learn how to sort, and store information to make it most useful. Often it is more temperament and socialisation that restricts them moving across the invisible line between information and knowledge workers.

Data workers are the semi-skilled workers who have little intrinsic engagement with their task. Whereas in the past it was brawn and not brain that was valued, now it is more likely to be simply boredom toleration. Farm workers became factory workers – sort of semi-automatons who tended what Dickens called the 'melancholy mad elephants' in the 'dark satanic mills'. Today, they may be seen in cleaner, quieter, brightly lit environments tied to computer screens. Many monitor events passively; others input stuff that they have little affinity with.

A number of things determine where one fetches up in the system. In the old days, origins pretty much determined destination. Parental class and education pretty well determined adult social class with the middle class of last century. Ability played an important factor when free education was introduced, particularly when education opportunities were linked to ability through selection such as in grammar schools. At all stages, personality and values played a part. Parents have always attempted to socialise values into their children, like postponement of gratification, achievement striving, helping others. Study both very successful scientists (i.e. Nobel prize winner) and very successful entrepreneurs (top 100 business people), and one is struck by patterns in the early upbringings of both groups. Some are driven 'to know', others 'to have'. Some appear to have an insatiable, unstoppable drive and energy to achieve, others are much more laid back. At extremes, neither are very interested in a work-life balance, the one group fulfil themselves primarily through work, the other through leisure. These motivational drivers are often a mix between ability, personality and parental/school socialisation.

But these days, class mobility seems greater not only up the ladder but down it as well. Just as we saw the millennium internet bubble expand and pop creating and then destroying multi-million-pound companies in months, so technology can change information workers into data workers and data workers into an employment underclass.

The new technology will always allow the talented and dedicated to rise. Even the low emotionally intelligent, technical wizard can make a fortune out of the power of applying new ideas. The data worker's child may overnight become a knowledge worker – something unheard of in previous times with social class mobility being very slow. However, the reverse pattern can be equally swift and unpredictable. How the mighty can fall!

It is not that class is not important anymore; or even that the distinctions are not clear. But mobility is now more possible than ever – even in 'class-ridden' societies like Britain and India.

Lies at work

There is a lot of interest in integrity testing in the business world because most managers are conscious of the consequences of people who habitually lie. Thus, hapless interviewees may be subject to curious questionnaires or even a lie detector type test to show their honesty. (see page 107)

But the selectors themselves rarely think about the official lying that goes on in the organisation. Perhaps like Party Political Broadcasts, we are simply used to hearing one-sided, carefully packaged sound bites and disregard them. Maybe we see internal memos emanating from the top as sort of advertorials for the organisation rather than genuine communication.

One of the characteristics of psychopaths is that they are unable to know (or care about) fact and fiction; truth and lies; reality and imagination. Some organisations collectively behave like that. Both internal and external communication is a blatant lie about it.

Some of the more common porkies get into the culture. They are 'borrowed' by others such that everybody uses them. They become part of everyday business babble – a strange tongue that takes time to master. Linguistically, its closest other languages are psychobabble and porky-pie-speak.

Perhaps a bored employee could do us all a favour and do some serious research into the area. First, they would need to expand on the above to make the list comprehensive. Second, they might like to ascertain the popularity of various porkies: those waning and those waxing in the firmament. Third, they may like to note those that are the favoured porkies of IT consultants and what do lawyers or insurance companies use. Last, but most important of all, we need a translation – a sort of porky-truth dictionary. This means stating what the porkie really means for those charmingly young and naive people who have just come into the organisation. It may even seem to make some porkies politically incorrect? You know, there may even be a PhD in this for someone.

Cynicism in organisations, like prejudice in public, has been 'privatised'. Only at dinner parties with trusted friends can one say what one really believes about certain issues like religion, politics – and business.

People have learnt never to challenge the Pravda-like statement emitting from the board. It can be too career limiting.

For some cynics, the more a business proclaims various slogans, the more likely they are to ignore them. It's a bit like countries: if a country calls itself the 'Free Democratic People's Republic of …' you can be pretty certain it's neither free nor democratic.

Consider the following classic porkies:

Lies about Appraisal and Promotion

- Fundamentally, individual performance (not service) will be rewarded.
- I will review your performance every 6 months.
- You will be promoted strictly on merit.
- You are the only one not to have conducted the appraisals on time.
- The salary structure is competitive, bench-marked and on par with Industry Averages.

Lies about Communication

- All senior managers have an open-door policy.
- Please be honest: we never shoot the messenger of bad news.
- This organisation is refreshingly free of hearsay and rumours.
- We will take your most pressing question at the end.
- Mr Curruthers is in a meeting and will return your call.
- We value open and honest discussions on all issues.
- Your boss holds no secrets about the future organisation.

Lies about Training

- Training is, and will remain, our highest priority.

- Training ensures that there is no favouritism among appraisers.
- Older employees particularly enjoy the opportunity to retrain.
- We will never cut the training budget in times of recession.
- All our trainers are up-to-date, business-oriented professionals.

Lies about Restructuring

- You will probably be better off under the new structure.
- Our future is particularly bright.
- Our major reason for restructuring is to be more flexible for our customers.
- Business re-engineering is not about downsizing.
- This merger will not lead to redundancies.

Lies about Service

- Your customer feedback is important to how we operate.
- Customer alignment is not about laying people off.
- We are a totally customer-focused business.
- We pride ourselves in fully understanding our customers needs and wants.

Lies about Innovation

- We reward risk-takers in this organisation
- We believe innovativeness is common in our organisation
- Employees are all encouraged to take their own decisions and innovate in their own way
- We are not afraid of creative disagreement
- We are all creative: we just need to find out how to liberate it

Looking at oneself and others

Being good at business means being shrewd, insightful and perspicacious. There are many ways in which one needs to be perceptive: sensitive to market trends, aware of competitors and particularly responsive to staff issues.

But how self-aware does one need to be? All the enthusiasm for the concept of emotional intelligence no doubt reflects the fact that perceptiveness and sensitivity are as important as what Americans call 'smarts' in business.

Psychologists have distinguished between (at least) three types of social perception: *self-perception, other-perception* and *meta-perception*. You need to be pretty good at all three really to succeed at work.

Dictionaries of psychological terminology are stuffed full of 'self' words: self-abasement; self-absorption; self-consciousness; self-control; self-deception; self-denial; self-esteem; self-expression; self-monitoring. Indeed there is a branch of the discipline called Self Psychology.

How we see ourselves is fundamentally important to healthy psychological function. Ask any therapist; look at any self-help bookshelf. The central question is about the accuracy of **self-perception**, particularly the perception of ability, personality, physique and motivation. How biased are people in their self concepts? Do they over- or under-rate themselves, or are they pretty accurate?

The problem of course, lies in measuring the accuracy of people's perceptions. This is difficult to do objectively, though there are some interesting methods. For instance, the way experts measure body-image distortion in anorexia, bulimics and the grossly obese, is to get them to stand in front of a distorting mirror. The mirror may be concave or convex to make the reflection appear 'taller-and-thinner' or 'shorter-and-fatter' than is the case in reality. The odd-shaped person standing in front of the mirror (preferably naked but if not, in tight figure-hugging clothing) has an electronic keyboard that actually allows them to bend the mirror. Their task is to bend it until it is 'straight' or '180º' - that is, that they perceive the reflection to be accurate. They are given as long as they need to do this. The task is repeated many times beginning at a different deliberately distorting point. The experiment similarly measures the angle of the mirror that the patient says is accurate. This tells both the degree and direction of distortion.

Of course it is not as easy to measure all aspects of individuals. Abilities, specifically intelligence, are fairly straight forward to measure accurately, though there are those who argue that intelligence and ability are impossible to measure. They are blinkered and deluded and may be trying to hide something. Personality is also measurable, though there are additional problems of people dissimulating or not being able accurately to report on their motives and needs.

Many people suffer from low self-esteem. They under estimate their IQ and EQ and their physical and interpersonal attractiveness. Therapists, trainers and managers often have a real battle trying to shift those seemingly illogical and self-defeating beliefs that can be self-fulfilling. Believe you can't do something and you don't try – or succeed in proving yourself right in the first place.

Whilst the most common self-perception distortion is to under-rate yourself, there are a small number who have the opposite pattern. They believe, despite the evidence, that they are more attractive, charming and intelligent than they are. How they come to be that way is often found in their childhood, but their self-confidence may have been usefully self-fulfilling.

However, the positive bias can have down sides. It can lead to unrealistic goal setting and poor coping strategies when rejection occurs.

The second type of perception is the accurate **perception of others**. Some people are quite simply more perceptive than others. They read the signals, pick up the cues, read the data – and they correctly infer the other person's needs, emotional state and motives.

Some call it 'intuition', others 'emotional intelligence' and still others 'sensitivity', but they are all talking about the same thing. Most people prefer face-to-face feedback so that they can read the body language of their interlocutor. They say that, to fully understand the other person, they need to see them.

But what is it that makes one person both more sensitive and accurate at perceiving others than another? Certainly, experience plays a big part; particularly the experience of power. To use old-fashioned terminology, servants have to be more perceptive of, and sensitive toward, the foibles and moods of the master than vice versa. They know to be hyper-alert and responsive when the master is in a bad mood, but to exploit him when in a good mood. The experience of ducking and diving teaches a great lesson.

Neurotics are often remarkably sensitive to the pain of others but unable to deal with it. And that's the rub of being very perceptive. Real social skill involves both being insightful enough to know what is going on psychologically but also, where necessary, doing something about it. That is, it is all very well knowing that a person is upset, but it's also quite important to know how, when and why to comfort them. In this sense being perceptive can carry a cost.

We all know the remarkably insensitive person – usually a male, often a techie – who claims, quite honestly, not to have noticed that a report was severely depressed, frequently drunk or upset and vengeful. It is quite amazing how people can ever get to the state of being quite so imperceptive of others. But we all know that it occurs – all too frequently, alas.

The third type of perception is **meta-perception**, which is your perception of their perception of you. You can, if you wish, play with the concept of meta-meta perception. It is the stuff of marriage counselling, public-speaking and interviews. It is in effect being sensitive to the impression you are making.

We all become aware of the impression we are having on others. They maybe bored or frightened, intrigued or anxious, puzzled or amused. A lot of the time, people try to hide their real reactions. Ask a friend what they think of your new hair cut, or tie, or dress, and they nearly all struggle to find a compliment. However, those with good meta-perception are able to detect the real reaction of the person.

Marital counselling is often for people with poor meta-perception. Partners may be unable either to send or receive accurate messages about their wants and desires. They are unable to read reactions to their behaviour.

The stand-up comic and the after-dinner speaker certainly need good meta-perception. They need to judge how they are coming across and to adapt their performance accordingly. Ideally, lecturers, teachers and trainers should have the same skill, though many don't.

And like other people, it can be paralysing and frustrating when one is meta-perceptively sensitive but interpersonally or performance-wise, gauche. True skill is about changing your act to get the result you want – if, of course, you read the signals correctly.

So the moral of the story is this. To be socially perceptive, aware, flexible and skilled, you need to have accurate self-, other- and meta-perception. But to be thought of as really socially skilled, you need to be able to change your behaviour to the feedback you receive.

M

Managerial courage

What appears to be one of the barmier management training techniques involves people walking over hot coals. The 'trick' of Hindu holy men can be done in Hastings, Hounslow or Highgate. And the purpose and message of this potentially painful and dangerous act: management is really mostly about courage.

It is part of the same message that is at the heart of outdoor training. The idea is that management is as much about the heart as the head. That people need each other to survive – literally, as you ford rivers and cross ravines. And also, as importantly, you learn more from experiential training than conceptual training.

Potholes work better than power point; mountains better than manuals; bush-walking better than breakout groups. There is a lot to learn in becoming a competent business manager – about strategy, technology, accounting and appraisal. One can even learn the soft skills necessary for counselling and negotiation. But there are a few things one does not learn in business school or in the boardroom – courage, balls, guts. Business courage is not that different from battle courage: it is surprising who does and does not manifest it, when and why.

Reading obituaries of courageous medal-holders, it is not always clear what drove them to conspicuous acts of gallantry. Often they were motivated primarily by care of their fellow men more than hatred of the enemy. Occasionally it is about taking well-calculated risks. And sometimes it is more about luck.

There are at least three types of courage needed in business. The first is the **courage to fail**. It is the courage to try something new; to experiment; to buck the trend; to take risk. It takes confidence and self-belief. With failure comes humiliation, recrimination and a broken reputation.

For many managers the cost to themselves (let alone others) is simply too great. They may have a really good idea about product innovation, process re-engineering or even man-management, but the fear of getting it wrong means they do nothing. They let others win the prizes.

Courage to fail and judicious risk assessment are not the same thing. One can make an excellent risk calculation but, on the same data set, some will and some will not act. Lack of courage may be the result of low confidence, a very conservative mentality, and pressure from home. Others go in for so much analysis (to be sure), it all ends in analysis paralysis with nothing being done.

The courage to fail is the courage to be first, to try something new, to be ahead of your time; to trust your instincts; to be creative – knowing it could all go very wrong.

Perhaps the most important and neglected courage is **interpersonal courage**. It's the sort of courage it takes to confront the employee with BO; or to make people redundant. More than assertiveness and counselling are involved here. It's the courage to deal with others' raw emotions; to say what needs to be said; to show compassion; even to be strong by being weak.

Appraisal systems fail because managers can't tell people their performance is average. Turnover gets out of hand because work-place bullies are not confronted or the aggressively hypochondriacal are not warned. The more intellectual the managers or the culture, the less comfortable they are around emotions of any sort.

Big, strong, tough men are usually worst at this. 'The British' remarked Sir Michael Edwards, 'seem so courageous in war, but so pusillanimous in peace'. This remark had much to do with confronting the unions or activists like 'Red Robbo'. But it also has to do with confronting people whose personal pathology has made life miserable and inefficient for many: the secretary to the CEO and the safety officer who discover they can exercise tremendous power over those more senior than themselves and block productive work; the attention-seeking neurotics who make sure all around them obey curious rules to make them happy; the back-stabbing inadequates, angry for being 'passed over', who in effect work to rule; the HR people whose personal counselling obsessions mean they are in effect doing a different (and inappropriate) job compared to the one they were hired for. They all need to be confronted – directly, quickly and fairly.

And you will be surprised at the number of captains-of-industry who can't face all that 'emotional stuff'. Some have favoured henchmen for the task – or henchwomen, as women often seem much better at this. Indeed, women always seem more interpersonally sensitive and courageous than men. Studies on dying patients have shown that it is not the clever (male) oncologists who unambiguously tell the patients their fate, but rather the (female) night nurses. Often female process consultants can say things to an all-male board that no man can. That is emotional courage.

The third type of courage is **moral courage**: the courage to stand up for a set of moral beliefs when in the ethical quicksands of modern-day business. Senior managers are confronted every day with moral dilemmas, challenges and – temptation. It involves the courage to refuse a senior colleague's appointing his or her spouse or children to the job others are better suited to (nepotism). It involves setting a strict, open and reasonable policy on receiving gifts of all sorts and at all levels. The 'fact-finding mission' may be as prone to bribery as a hamper at Christmas.

Often the hardest task is drawing the line in the mercurial world of business where so many appear to be disregarding the rules; bending the guidelines; ripping people off. It is the courage of Bonhoffer or Wallenberg. It is the courage not to give in to or turn a blind eye to wrong-doing. It may be about little else than ensuring fairness.

But in the world of moral relativism, it is all too easy to remain silent. It takes courage for the parent to inform the social security that their excellent, caring but deceiving nanny is claiming unemployment benefit. It takes courage to take a real stand against the forces of darkness.

Curiously, few companies have courage as a core competency. They may have ideas about assertiveness, negotiation and risk taking but courage is more than this. Churchill and Thatcher were courageous – but also difficult to deal with. It can make leaders seem fanatical and intolerant. And of course the line between courageous and pig-headed is often fine.

But there remain many companies eternally grateful to the CEO who has all three aspects of courage mentioned above: courage to fail, to confront, to uphold principle. And it can be the most unlikely of people who do and don't manifest it. For some, they only take courage when the chips are really down, but for others it is a really enduring characteristic.

Managing the under-performer

Managing the demotivated, unco-operative, negative, irritable, frequently absent employee is what is called on training courses, a challenge. To have only conscientious, motivated, talented peers and reports is as joyful as it is rare. It is therefore, in training-speak, a developmental opportunity to learn how to manage the under-performer.

The ability to 'deal with' and cope with, let alone 'cure', the under-performer is a major management skill. Sour, demotivated people can poison their peers. They tend to get 'dug in' and deeply resistant to all management attempts to improve their performance. In some jobs, whose outcome measures are clearly specifiable, it can be relatively straightforward to deal with the under-performer. It is easier to persuade a poor performer to leave or improve if you have the data.

In some call centres these days, everyone is electronically monitored (number of calls per day; revenue per call, etc). Some even have their chairs monitored (by heat or weight) - you can't be selling unless you are at your desk (with the headphones on). In this sense, one can challenge poor output on a daily basis if you have proof; but most of us, alas, do not.

The fault of most managers is that they look for solutions before they understand the cause. Many are brought up with the 'fix it' mentality of action man. They think of training courses, sabbaticals, even personal counselling. Some try and redeploy problem under-performers in another part of the organisation – send them to the stores, or HR, or catering management. One CEO had the brilliant idea of herding them all together in a prestigious sounding subsidiary and then selling it off.

What are the classic signs of under-performance? They tend to relate to time keeping, mood states and focus. Under-performers suffer from both absenteeism and presenteeism. They like to escape as much as possible and equate being present with doing work. They are also moody, irritable, critical, quick to fly off the handle and passive-aggressive. They have almost nothing positive to say about others and live in a world of sniping at the happy, contented, and productive worker.

Most of all they lose their enthusiasm and focus. They somehow remove their heart and brain before starting work only to relocate and re-activate them after work. They represent the 'quit-but-stay' old dogs of the organisation.

So how does one diagnose the cause of the problem. The answer is no different from that of your GP. Imagine a person going to a doctor complaining of a headache. Traditionally the GP asks a series of set questions: when did it first occur; how long did it last; what pattern did it take; had it ever occurred before? Essentially they are questions about duration, frequency, intensity and unusualness, given the medical condition of the person. By doing so, they may be able to determine whether the cause was anything as varied as stress, a brain tumour or hidden alcoholism.

Symptoms lead to questions that lead to diagnosis and thence attempts to find a solution. Solutions maybe as varied as warnings and sackings to offers of counselling or training.

Jobs change: they become more complex and the technology that needs to be mastered is forever being upgraded. People have to be bright enough for a job. Too bright and they get bored but not bright enough and they become stressed, change-averse and uncooperative. It is not a favourable diagnosis but an important one – some people under-perform because they are not bright enough to learn to adapt quickly enough.

And there are no easy solutions to this problem. Training courses don't make people more intelligent. In fact they serve to expose those who are not bright enough. Those who, through lack of ability, can't hack the job need to be 'let go' - not passed on to personnel where they can do more damage. Demotion, early retirement or a lesser part-time job are best solutions. They need to be helped not to lose face but they need work more compatible with their abilities.

People under-perform because they have not been trained to do it. The training has been absent, poor, too quick, too long ago and/or not supported in the work place. It is a common problem particularly where there is a change in structure, equipment, customer needs or the like. Under-performance can be fairly easily cured if a judicious choice of courses are chosen and supported. In some organisations training is seen as a reward – a jolly time at a nice hotel. In others it is a punishment and the mark of Cain to peers. It should, and need not, be either. Skills need to be acquired and practiced in a changing world. More importantly, the organisation needs to reward skills acquisition – not punish it, leading to deep cynicism about the whole enterprise.

There are three other important causes of under-performance, alongside lack of ability and training. The first is distraction – people have things going on in their lives, which means they take their eye off the ball. It maybe an affair, sickness in the family or more worryingly, some form of addiction – alcohol, drugs, gambling. The symptoms are secrecy (lots of phone calls), poor time keeping, moodiness, increasing absenteeism. And the solution? Support first; deadlines second. That is, people often need help – time off, counselling and so on, but they need to be told there is a deadline by which time further steps will need to be taken if things are not going well.

Another problem is simple personality. People selected for a particular trait may soon be shown to have too much of it. The bold and confident young man might be hiding his narcissism. The diligent, careful, meticulous workers chosen for their conscientiousness may soon expose themselves as total neurotic compulsives. The agreeable and compliant person may turn out to be totally dependent. The clever sceptic may turn out to be paranoid just as the creative turns out to be utterly unreliable and totally impractical. The excitable, amazing and enthusiastic creative may soon reveal that those traits are simply driven by powerful underlying neurons.

The quietly reserved person may later reveal him or herself as indifferent and deeply uncommunicative. Equally the easy going may simply reveal themselves to be passive aggressive. The problem is that people present the best side of their personality at interview. Often one can have 'too much of a good thing' which leads to problems.

Therapy for difficult staff members maybe too costly. Again the best solution is to terminate the contract. People with non-optimal traits can be 'managed-back' to being production workers but don't kid yourself that it is easy.

There is a fifth and final cause of under-performance. And that may be the way in which the person has been managed in the past. The corporate culture management style can and does have a massive impact on employee motivation and performance. Management is about challenge and support: bosses need to set clear, attainable but stretching goals for employees and then help them attain them. Goal setting is often done badly – people are not set them or they are impossible to achieve. Both situations are deeply stressful and lead to under-performance. Equally one may have a very supportive and kind boss who does not push one to achieve, so little is done.

When people have worked in one organisation all their lives, they believe what they are experiencing is normality. Those who change jobs become painfully and immediately aware of issues like corporate culture and all sorts of subtle norms about dress, time keeping, expected productivity. Those going from public to private sector or from organisational to self-employment often have a great surprise. They then, and often only then, become aware of how the management style in their previous organisation impacted on their and their colleagues' behaviour.

Normal, healthy, well-chosen and enthusiastic staff can become alienated, uncommitted under-performers through the way in which they are managed. These under-performers need 're-enthusing'. They need clear goals, lots of support and positive colleagues. They can, as Mao believed, be re-educated for the new order!

In other words the source of the under-performance lies not in the employee but in the way in which they are managed. The fault therefore, dear manager may lie not in your employees but in yourself!

Managing the customer-facing employee

Business gurus have been quick to highlight and indeed embellish a few not-very-well-conducted studies, which have claimed to show that customer service is a function of management style. The argument goes that the way service staff deal with their customers reflects clearly how they themselves are managed. The attitudes, behaviour and emotions that employees express to customers reflect their own feelings to their work, and these sentiments are determined by their managers. Employees 'leak their attitudes', spilling them onto customers. Customers 'catch' employee attitudes through emotional contagion. This leads, in short, to the belief that employee morale is closely, directly and positively related to customer service satisfaction.

Researchers have pointed out that even employees' own perceptions of their service quality are related to both their personal job satisfaction and productivity. They could, of course, simply be deluded. But the theory has three axioms:

1. When organisations treat their employees well, they treat their customers accordingly.
2. When organisations and the work group have policies and practices that are really concerned with service quality, customers will be happier with those services.
3. The more their employees have actual contact with customers, the more their morale and organisational policies affect customer satisfaction.

A 'jobsworth' manager models jobsworth attitudes to the staff who are, in turn, inattentive and unhelpful. By contrast, the caring and sharing manager has staff who model exemplary customer service. The idea is that somehow the corporate culture and predominant management style can be appraised by contact with often the most lowly members of that company.

It was for this reason a now-forgotten management guru talked about the upside-down organisation. The theory was this: the customer is king and therefore needs superb treatment by service staff. Staff at the customer interface need to be supported, trained and directed by their supervisors to ensure high quality service. All people in the organisation should be directed to this end. So the CEO's job is to help, support and advise the board, whose job it is to help, support and advise their senior managers. We are therefore all support staff attempting to support the most important staff who have contact with those that pay their salary – the customer.

Simplified, evangelical guru-speak or radical, insightful management? All service organisations invest in trying very hard to get excellent customer service. Airlines, hotels, restaurants and the like conduct serious selection and training to get the sort of person who enjoys, and thrives at, customer service. Stable, optimistic extroverts of sufficient, though not sparkling, intellect seem ideal. They rely on many courses, feedback and incentives to keep up standards. And they are aware of the role of modelling good behaviour.

But managers in the service industry also know that other factors, beyond their control, affect staff morale, mood and service. Irascible, demanding, downright rude customers can sap the morale of staff, no matter how well they are treated by their managers. It has been said that customer service is emotional labour on a par with physical labour. There is the same amount of exhaustion. And as customers demand more and more for less and less, the customer-facing staff bear the brunt.

Equally, whatever the quality, or amount in the work-life balance, we all have private lives which impinge on work lives. Many customer service jobs involve young(ish) people. And people of a particular age and stage have particular problems. Relationships, money worries, young children – they all radically impact on mood and attitude at work, irrespective of training, management support or whatever. Service staff are not very well paid and can also be exposed to other temptations, like easy accessibility of alcohol. There are plenty of distractions – which all lead to problems. Happy-go-lucky service staff may be particularly prone to dabbling in a little of the lifestyle of their cosseted customers – and this can lead to serious problems in the long or short term.

The customer-focused organisation and manager may, in extremes, lead the company to ruin. Being too eager to please may lead to delighted customers and a bankrupt company. Further, some managers may not be sufficiently innovative in anticipating what might please customers as opposed to giving them what they currently want.

Yes, happy staff are better with their customers. But this is a bit like the spurious assumption between satisfaction and productivity. This question is essentially the direction of causality. Are happy employees more productive, or are productive workers more satisfied? Or is the relationship reciprocal? Or is it epiphenomenal, because both are controlled by another variable, like personality? Thus it could be – and there is evidence on this – that extroverts are intrinsically more happy and also (in service jobs) intrinsically more productive.

The trouble with the happy-employee-happy-customer theory is that it is, quite simply, too simple. Things are a bit more complicated than that. Many things determine employees' morale on the job (their personalities, their relationships, their health, the health of the economy). And many things determine customer satisfaction.

Customers are by definition very different in their wants, likes, needs. That is why the idea of consumer groups who speak on behalf of (all) customers is preposterous. They are unelected 'behalfers'; pressure groups who, unelected, speak on behalf of others whom they never consult. Some customers are easy to please; for others, satisfaction is, in effect, impossible. Any employee knows this.

This, of course, does not mean that employee morale is not important; that managers should not model the service they want; and that organisations should not have clear, dynamic and seriously applied service quality policies and practices. But it is naive to believe that these factors alone will do the trick at the customer interface.

N

Natural history of management fads

What ever happened to quality circles and management seminars? And what about all that enthusiasm for empowerment re-engineering? Does your boss still 'manage by wandering about', or is that a thing of the past? Can you recite your company vision, departmental mission or personal job statement, or is that all old hat?

Management is notoriously faddish as stressed and troubled managers try to find cheap, quick and effective solutions to their intractable problems. Like overweight adults, they seek one miracle cure after another, seeming never to have learnt that they do not exist. The celery diet, the hip and thigh diet, the protein diet – all promise more than they can deliver and get quickly forgotten.

1 – Academic Discovery

Other faddish ideas can be traced to the stuffy and distinctly unfaddish world of academia. A modest discovery may result in a pretty indigestible paper. Traditionally, these papers show the causal link between two factors relevant to work situations. But these papers are not only dry and complicated, but they are cautious. There are a lot of 'perhaps', 'notwithstanding', 'towards'. Academics often call for replication, more research, they are hesitant and underline the complexity of all the actual and possible factors involved. And few are interested in immediate application. Their job is understanding the process, not changing the world.

2 – Description of the Study

This process can last a long time, and usually involves a lot of elaboration and distortion in the process. Someone reads the paper and provides a summary. The summary may be verbal and if so may end a little like Chinese whispers. Often the discovery is mentioned in a brainy presentation. Others hear it and repeat it. But with every repetition, the findings become stronger and the complexity weaker. Selective memory ensures that the crucial findings are recorded and embellished. At this stage, it is unlikely that the researcher would recognise the findings as theirs in the first place.

3 – Popularisation in a Best Seller

The next stage is the big one. A business writer/guru takes up the call, hears about the finding, gives it a catchy title and before you know what, the fad is about to begin. That one single and simple idea soon became a book. Indeed, that is why business books are so easy to read and precise, there is really very little in them. The best seller with a snappy title, publisher hype and the rest, mean that the average manager at least reads a few reviews of the book. He or she may even buy it, but many are content to hear the gist from reviewers. And they are frequently envious of seemingly powerful results that occur when the great idea is followed. It is at this stage that the fad becomes a buzzword.

4 – Consultant Hype and Universalisation

It is not the academic or the author that really powers the fad but an army of management consultants trying to look as if they are at the cutting edge of management theory. Because the concepts are easy to understand and are said to have wide application, the consultants seek to apply them everywhere. And the word spreads like wildfire.

Soon it seems everyone has to be empowered, re-engineered, 360°ed, etc. Those who don't climb aboard are made to feel left out, fuddy-duddy, even bad for their shareholders.

5 – Total commitment by true believers

At this point, the evangelists move from the consultants to the managers. For a small number of companies, the technique seems to have brought quick, massive benefits. They become happy and willing product champions, which only serves to sell more books and fan the fires of faddishness.

With hindsight, it is sometimes difficult to explain why the effect had such an impact on the view. Psychologists often explain this in terms of the Hawthorne effect or placebo effect. The former refers to the way people react positively when they are treated differently (irrespective of what the treatment consists of) while the latter refers to the sugar pill effect, where simply believing that it will do you good is enough.

In fact, years after the fad had passed, there are little outstations of believers who continue to be the faithful. In time, they are quiet reminders of the past as they cling on. The Amish of management, they resolutely cling on to their old ways.

6 – Doubt, Scepticism, Cynicism and Defection

After pride comes the fall. After a few years of heavy product selling, the appetite for the fad becomes diminished. The market is saturated. Various 'new and improved' or just as likely 'shorter and simpler' versions of the fad are introduced. But it is apparent that the enthusiasm is gone.

And then the avalanche or mudslide begins. It begins with managerial doubt and then academic scepticism, followed by journalistic cynicism, and finally consultant defection. It may be that the whole process starts with people pointing out the poor cost-benefit analysis of introducing the fad. Or it may occur because someone goes back to the original finding and shows that the gap has widened so much between what was initially demonstrated and what is now done, that the two are different species.

Then management journalists smell blood. It is easy to find disaffected managers happy to squeal. They point out the thousands spent for little reward and the incredible consultant rip-off the whole thing has become. A trickle becomes a stream and then a river. And the consultants who were so eager to pick up the fad are the first to drop it. What gave them both credibility and massive invoicability now makes them look like con-artists as they distance themselves from the fad.

7 – New Discoveries

The end of one fad is an ideal time for trainers, writers and consultants to spot a gap in the market. They know there is an incurable thirst for magic bullet, fix-all solutions, so the whole process starts again. The really clever people begin to sense when the previous fad is reaching its sell-by date, so that they have just enough time to write their new best seller to get the market just right.

How long does the typical fad last? It depends on the zeitgeist; whether there is a bull or bear market and on the entrepreneurial hunger of authors and consultants. But what is clear is that there are as many middle-aged fashion victims as young ones.

O

On being average

With few exceptions, all human characteristics from bra to brain-size, and height to hearing are normally distributed. Everything, not just intelligence, is a bell-curve. And because we know a lot about the statistical properties of a bell-curve, we 'know' most of us are average on most things. The trouble is when others tell us that this is so.

What the bell-curve shows is that around 68% of us fall between a standard deviation above or below the norm. In IQ terms that is 85 and 115: in height for men it's probably around 5 foot 5 to 6 foot; in bra size, it's probably 34 to 38. And 96% of the population lie between two standard deviations: in IQ terms 85 to 130. A few are really bright and a similar number really dim. Most of us are average on most things – alas!

Sometimes it's a relief being told one is average. Most middle-aged baby boomers react positively to being told that their sex life is average, which can also mean normal. But for generation-X, brought-up on a rich diet of self-esteem improvement, being told one is average as opposed to extra-ordinary, special, very talented – is not so wonderful.

However, there is one area of life where the bell-curve rarely rings true and that is in the world of appraisal. Curiously, this is despite the fact that we know that most work-related human abilities are normally distributed. Consider the typical 5-point rating scale designed by HR for progress reviews and performance appraisal. Typically 5 will be described as 'outstanding' (or other superlatives like 'exceptional performance'); 4 as 'above standard'; 3 as 'meets standards'; 2 as 'below standards'; and 1 as 'well-below standards'. If work performance were a bell-curve we would know exactly how many of each number we would find.

But everyone knows from experience that this never happens. The five-point scale becomes, in effect, a three-point scale because numbers 2 and 1 are so rarely used. Organisations are aware of this and try to deal with it in one of three ways:

The rarest, most draconian and least successful is the forced distribution method. In effect, this forces the bell-curve by giving the rater a specific number of 1s, 2s, 3s, 4s, and 5s that he or she can use. If they 'run-out' of 4s they have to use 3s etc. Managers hate this because they are forced to differentiate, which has implications for giving negative feedback, which is what they really hate most of all.

The second method is to change the labels. So one has nearly all positive rating labels indicating above average: only the lowest score suggests below average; or may even suggest average itself. Thus the message is that the worst you can be is average. This is the favoured approach, particularly where the culture is litigious. This is a test of feedback by euphemism: a language spoken with unselfconscious eloquence by special relationship, transatlantic, ex-colonial friends. Weaknesses used to be called developmental opportunities for the skill-challenged. Now they are called latent strengthettes! The trouble with this method is that we soon run short of descriptives for Stakhanovite Wunderkinds. The descriptors can also sound very hollow to the sceptical supervisor who actually works with these average but positive-feedback-hungry souls.

The third method is to widen the scale. If a 5-point scale effectively becomes a three-point scale, then theoretically a seven-point scale becomes five points, nine becomes 6 or 7 etc. Whilst this is usually true, scale constructors run out of labels for a 10 point scale. And there is the problem of words not matching numbers: is the difference between exceptional and strong (performance) the same as between average and weak? This method taxes the form constructors' verbal skills too much and is soon abandoned.

And all this fuss is about having to tell someone the truth: that much of their performance at work and much of their behaviour (attitude, skill, output) is average. We all want to believe in Lake Woebegone, 'Where all the women are strong and the men are good looking and the children are all above average'. But if Lake Woebegone is a reasonable size, the truth must out: some women are strong but most are average and some men are handsome but others ugly and alas only about half of the children are above average.

Differentiating feedback works well. To be given poor ratings is an excellent warning or wake-up call for the serious under-performer. He or she may 'buck up their ideas', increase effort or look for another job. Unless the rating is biased or the employee deluded, the well-below standard, serious-deficiency feedback is an excellent yellow card. Top ratings only work well if they are accurate but unique. Satisfaction from a top score is soon evaporated if one discovers others have similar ratings: further, a top score has to be matched by rewards like money, promotion or some other valued perk.

The problem lies for that middle group of 2/3 to 3/4 of employees who are pretty average. They are okay, average, middle-of the-road. Most are the backbone, mainstay, heart of the company. But vanity and pride and what the Chinese call 'face' means that people do not enjoy giving or getting that message. Of course, the message is often harder to give because it is tied to monetary reward – the most tangible sort of feedback.

So raters come up with well-rehearsed and familiar lines explaining why they do not or cannot ('in all honesty') give the statistically expected number of average ratings. They include: 'My people are actually above average' - meaning both company and population standards. After all, we selected them; and they work for the world famous 'Acme Widgets' so they must be better than average. Another approach apes the funny way Oxford dons used to have wonderfully fine distinctions: 'alpha + – –' which is subtly worse than 'alpha + + –'. So by making fine distinctions 'within' the average category, one can, paradoxically, ban the concept of average.

The third method of trying to avoid the 'I think you are average' feedback is currently very popular. It's the 360-degree method whereby employees are not only rated by their boss, but also by their colleagues, subordinates, clients, customers – anybody, in fact, who knows them. Here the feedback given can say you are average because the manager is simply the messenger of a large group, not personally responsible for the rating. If 'everybody' says you are average it must be true! Perhaps the popularity in 360-degree feedback lies partly in the way people can receive feedback about their averageness.

Interestingly, if people evaluate themselves on a whole range of characteristics, the results seem fairly consistent. People think they are slightly above average (about half to a full standard deviation) on all desirable characteristics: altruism, empathy, intelligence; and equally about the same amount below average on less desirable characteristics (dishonesty, jealousy etc.). It maybe psychologically healthy for the ego to maintain these beliefs but it partly explains reactions to feedback that does not fit that carefully constructed but fragile picture.

The self-esteem movement that originated in America and which has had a profound effect on school children and university students is bubbling through to the world of work. It is making it much more difficult for the honest appraiser to reveal the truth during any type of appraisal. Those who are used to, and expect, exclusively positive, above-average feedback react rather badly when given the unusual message – your work is average. The paradox is now that average is exceptional.

Organisational behaviour

Anyone who has experienced management education, be it a week-long seminar, a diploma or even a MBA, will have met 'Organisational Behaviour' or OB. It is the behavioural science of business.

But what is OB? A bastard non-discipline that receives the epithet 'studies' or an important, integrative, practical science? There is no doubt that OB mixes a number of the social sciences – primarily sociology and psychology with a reasonable dose of anthropology, economics and political science. Is this exotic cocktail a good idea?

Any disinterested critic of OB may be forgiven for finding it pretentious, painfully obvious, turgid humbug. Some have suggested that OB specialists are not bright enough to become psychologists nor know enough to be sociologists. So they hide under the leaky umbrella of OB at smart business schools, dishing up ideas nearly all derivative of the real academic disciplines. There is practically no idea, theory or method that has not been borrowed from psychology or economics. Does this mean there are necessarily no clever thinkers in the area? Perhaps, like the Japanese manufacturers, they are brilliant imitations of others. OB researchers and writers take good ideas, improve them and market them brilliantly.

But OB as a whole is incoherent and unsubstantive. The chapters in an OB book seem unconnected having little or nothing to do with one another. Topics can be arranged in any order. So OB researchers work on an enormous number of topics, each with many variables, unrelated to one another.

But when OB people come up with good ideas they don't confirm, expand or refute them. No school develops; no movement ensues even if the idea is good, the theory useful and the methodology innovative. When the topic gets difficult, the researchers move on, bored, to some 'cutting edge' new ideas. So OB becomes sort of specialist, highbrow news. It is desperately faddish.

There are more specific accusations that can be made against OB.

1. Political Correctness

This may involve anything from a doctrinaire denial of biological influences on human behaviour to laments about the fashionably oppressed. We need an intellectually honest history of OB and some realistic appraisal of why topics go in and out of fashion. OB seems particularly eager to jump on any politically correct bandwagon like diversity, espousing the accepted view. Fashion and acceptance, not veridicality, seem the important criteria for researching and writing about a topic.

2 – Anecdotes not data

There is too much on stories, case studies, parables and anecdotes and not enough emphasis on the data to substantiate theories and concepts. Medicine, like business, is eager to use case studies but it is (hopefully) an evidence-based discipline. Case studies make interesting reading and they are extremely useful for teaching. But in science we develop from hunch to hypothesis to theory to law. We move from observation and induction to verification and falsification. OB researchers need to develop and test theories more. Yes, it is a young science, but that is no excuse for slinking away from systematic data gathering to test theories.

3 – No powerful theories

A theory is a network of falsifiable causal generalisations. But OB has a messy stew of ideology, buzzwords and doctrinaire statements. What theory regularly leads to is the prediction of empirical relationships and generalisations across topics/phenomena. Theories in psychology and economics – dissonance theory, equity theory, social exchange theory – are warmly embraced but never bettered by OB theories. OB has lots of models which are boxes loosely connected with arrows but these are no substitute for real theories. We need theories of motivation and of organisational structure. We need, but do not have OB-generated, real theories of job stress and organisational structure.

4 – Derivative methodology

Most psychologists collect their own data to test hypotheses. And they choose the most appropriate methods to do so. Many economists analyse others' large data sets with sophisticated econometric models. OB does neither. The focus should be on what we know rather than how we found out about it. Methodology is a tool but an important one for doing research. OB research is difficult – there are lots of related and confounding factors but OB really needs to explore them sensitively and thoroughly.

5 – Identity

OB does not know what it is; and what it isn't. Its incoherence means it never rejects ideas, many of which are pretentious bunk (critical theory, grounded theory). Marxists, feminists, psychobiologists, ethnomethodologists all can find a cosy rest in OB. Everybody is welcome, all ideas are equally important; all approaches equally good. There are no rules, no limits, no quality control. All this exacerbates the identity problem.

6 – Marketing

OB people certainly know about marketing their ideas. Take the gurus of OB – Peters, Goleman, Handy. They know the power of the press; the virtue of spin and they use it to the full to further their cause. OB courses are well attended and OB departments are often highly rated within business schools because of the business that they attract. Marketing is important because often the ideas are ephemeral and vaporous – there is a constant need for marketing because there are constantly new products on the market.

7 – Attempting tractable rather important problems

OB people know the difference between those intractable but perennial problems of business that are pretty unsolvable. So they go for those pretty important things where they can make a difference. And this is a fairly good strategy. To make a small but significant difference is surely the right thing to do.

Journal and book authors need to state major findings clearly, free of organobabble, statistical jargon or ritualistic propitiations for long dead heroes of the revolution. What OB needs is some pretty simple things really: a set of criteria to determine success and failure; attempts to solve important problems of moderate difficulty; serious comparability to determine that one 'solution' is better than another.

Faced with a group of high-flying managers, one often notices a curious generational effect. The young Turks love technical solutions to all business problems and are deeply critical of all OB. Struggling, early-middle-aged managers are often obsessed by organisational structural issues, which drive them to look for solutions there. It is often the older and more powerful executives who know most problems at work are human relationship problems – and they are naturally, at least initially, attracted to OB, often to be disappointed.

P

Plural of anecdote is not evidence

What is the difference between a business case study and a biblical parable? A parable is defined as a narrative of imagined events used to illustrate a moral or spiritual lesson. All peoples have used allegories as a teaching aid to pass on the 'wisdom of the ancestors'. We may well be programmed to understand and remember by listening to and repeating stories with a particular structure.

The parable of the Good Samaritan, the widow's mite, the wedding at Canaan, the feeding of the five thousand, the prodigal son are brilliantly memorable. Indeed they are quoted by politicians when it suits them as they resonate deeply with those who know them.

And what of the case history so beloved of business school gurus? Why teach this way? There are many reasons for this choice of teaching method. They are adaptable and loosely based on real or imagined events. They can easily be updated, and made relevant to the time and place. Names, dates and figures can be changed; political correctness can be introduced; and outcomes can be manipulated to suit current sensitivities. In short they are easy to make realistic and relevant to any group.

Next, like good stories everywhere, they are often very memorable. They can be embellished and constructed in such a way to make them vivid or unusual. Through images, counter-intuitive outcomes, and the iconography of the age, case studies are designed to be easy to recall.

Case studies are also like inkblots or what psychologists call projective techniques. They may be, indeed must be, open to multiple interpretations;

paradoxically it is in their ambiguity that their power lies. They are complex poems to be read for nuances, subtle shades of meaning and quite different interpretations. In this sense, the interpretation depends as much on the insights and abilities of the reader as the content of the text.

Case studies are of course complex, or rather rich in images and outcomes. Even the most well known of biblical parables can be interpreted at various levels. Indeed the case studies often quite deliberately have data and evidence that lead up blind alleys. This is to encourage students to compete for the evidence.

And finally, the case study calls for participation. They are stimulants to debate and discussion. They are designed to start one off trying to decipher the causes, consequences and cures of various problems.

Case studies are used successfully in medicine and business to educate. Ideally, they supplement and complement the lecturing of facts, formulae, mechanisms, and processes. They bring things together, integrate learning, concretise the abstract.

But whereas medical and business academics use case studies, alternative and complementary medical practitioners and business consultants use anecdotes. An anecdote is a short account of an entertaining and interesting incident. It has none of the complexity of the case study but may be equally cavalier with the facts. And it nearly always has a positive outcome. Anecdotes of this kind are rich in pathos and may have a hint of bathos.

The etymology of the word anecdote suggests that it is about things unpublished. Things published usually have to be evaluated for their accuracy, for potential libels, for the quality of the writing and for the appropriateness of the inferences. All academic papers are scrupulously peer-reviewed for publication in an attempt to ensure their veridicality. The non-peer reviewed publication – worse the conference paper – is not considered serious work.

But some alternative practitioners and consultants are not in the business of scientific evidence; they are in the selling business. The same is true of many authors of business and health best sellers. They are packed with good stories – anecdotes about magic bullets, cures, of total recovery, of success and happiness.

And they come thick and fast from the lips of modern day snake-oil salesmen. They also come from the mouths of converts to this therapy, that management technique. And they represent what psychometricians call the 'fallacy of personal validation'; the idea that personal testimony, however sincere the anecdotalist, is not, nor can ever be, evidence of a technique working. Many cures are little more than placebo effects which themselves have also been shown to be powerful and persuasive.

Challenge the anecdotalist and they provide another anecdote. It is like listing the number of satisfied customers. The anecdotes are coherent and consistent in their bottom line and the assumption is that they provide evidence of proof. **The plural of anecdotes is not evidence**; it may be desperation.

Beware all consultants who provide only personal testimonials. Subjective validations are not sufficient evidence of proof unless accompanied by detailed, recorded observations. Many who testify are unaware of the forces acting upon them or their real needs and motives. It is imperative to examine the credibility of the source and this is more than diplomas and flash business cards.

The more a person is emotionally and financially committed to an issue, a product, a technique or a service, the more dubious they are. They neither welcome nor encourage rational, sceptical analysis. Negative unsuccessful cases are forgotten or go missing. Critics are dismissed as being immoral or dim.

Remember the burden of proof lies on the anecdotalists to prove their theories. They need to say what piece of evidence would disprove the theory. And they need to try a bit of alternative thinking, suggesting other explanations for the same phenomena. It is paradoxical indeed that those in alternative medicine seem so hostile to alternative thinking. And the same applies to management gurus who come up with radical, headline catching alternative management techniques.

Anecdotalists talk little of mechanisms or process. They are long on happy outcome and short on complex explanation. Beware the collection of heart rending, apple-pie anecdotes by a guru or a listing of happy customers. The collective noun for anecdotes is sales-pitch.

Psychometric fatigue

Since Bob Geldof talked about 'compassion fatigue' it has become popular to express a mixture of oversell and overkill of a message or product as XYZ-fatigue. A natural response to the message is to tune out, turn off – and yawn. One is fatigued not because the message is trivial or irrelevant but rather because it is repeated too often. Often one is bored and helpless – a pretty miserable mixture.

There is a new type of fatigue spreading through the system: psychological test fatigue. It is caused by five groups of people the first three of which are intimately involved with one another; human resource specialists, management consultants and test publishers. The other two also have an uncomfortable relationship; PR specialists and journalists. All have caused increasing test fatigue.

It is pretty unusual to go on any training course without having to complete some test that tells you about your style, your personality, or your preferred team role. Equally, newspapers and magazines are filled with merry typologies explaining everything from shopping types to gardening types. 'Are you a Demon or a Dodo under the Duvet? Turn to page 46 to find out'. These are tests of attitudes and beliefs, of preferences and traits; or learning style, thinking style and coping style. These are tests of real general intelligence, of emotional intelligence, of practical intelligence and of multiple intelligence. These are tests of normal as well as abnormal functioning. There are well designed and psychometrical tests, as well as those designed by journalists to amaze.

Why the enthusiasm for tests? Tests used by PR firms and their journalistic fellow travellers are more meant to amaze and entertain than instruct. There seems to be an insatiable desire for typologies. All products and product users can be typologised. Nothing is too trivial for this treatment. How you eat your cornflakes, how you decorate your office, how you choose wine, how you spend the weekend, how you cope with stress, how you choose your theatre seats, can all be put into amazing typologies. Journalists like them and PR people know it. They like a quiz (a polite word for a trivial test) to help people self-diagnose. But they are frankly unconcerned with accuracy – they simply want people to remember the brand name.

There are many reasons why trainers like tests. They argue, probably quite rightly, that people are not very sophisticated in their analysis and understanding of themselves or their peers. Tests can give people self-insight even if they reject what the test says. That is why there is more anxiety around ability tests than personality tests, which are seen to be both more accurate and having more important work-related implications.

Tests give comparative, specific and numerical data. Unlike references and testimonials, which flourish on euphemisms and double speak, tests give numeric data. One cannot get away with 'satisfactory', 'high spirited' and 'quirky' in tests. Good tests have normative data so you can measure yourself against population norms. And you can compare yourself to others on the course or in the organisation. Do you have above average EQ or only above average in your below average organisation? A good test could detect that.

But tests are most often used to educate in both language and process. The two are closely connected but alas a lot of the time they fail lamentably. And it is important to understand why. The idea is simple. People need to be educated in the language of individual differences. They need their vocabulary extended so that they can describe and understand people better. They need, in short, to be made more psychologically minded.

We have all heard that the Eskimos (Inuit) have 30 different words for snow reflecting their ability to subtly differentiate between forms of a substance pretty important to their daily lives. The argument goes that if you increase a person's psychological vocabulary, you increases their perceptiveness. But the theory breaks down mainly because typologies are about categorisation rather than understanding process. You can easily tell when people have been on too many courses: they know they are intuitors not sensors; they know in teams they are monitor evaluators and complete finishers; they know they have a reflective or pragmatic learning style; they might know they want more control (in their lives) than they show.

Often they have difficulty reconciling these different category systems. The language of different tests is incompatible. It is made all the more complex if they are fanatics about astrology, which is, of course, the prototype of all category systems. So they tend to remember the system that fits in best with their personal needs and forget all the rest. And the more alternative taxonomies they get, the more confused and fatigued they become.

The problem lies in the fact that categorisation per se does not explain process. It is important to know *why* a person is an extrovert or creative or sensitive – not just describe their characteristics. People are introverted or extroverted depending on their need for stimulation to maintain a particular level of arousal. People are creative because of their disinhibited associative system. People are sensitive because of their unstable mood swings.

Explain the mechanism and one understands the categorisation. It improves understanding and prediction.

Another problem with categorisation is that it often sets up false barriers or markers on a continuum. Most human characteristics, be they physical (i.e. height) or psychological (intelligence), are continuous, not categorical. Some are of course like eye colour or blood group, but that is fairly rare in psychological concepts. There is more or less: a bell-curve for intelligence, personality, and beliefs. One may talk in terms of types – introvert or extrovert but you must know there are extremes. People in the middle are ambiverts with characteristics of both; the extreme extrovert is a semi-maniac, seriously out-going, impulsive, sensation seeker, but his or her cousin a modest extrovert, may be social, assertive and optimistic – but not uncomfortably so.

Test taking is a drug for a few narcissists. For most people, it soon loses its power because it is as much confusing as entertaining; as much confusing as enlightening. If you are serious about using tests to improve your insight, choose one that has been psychometrically validated, based on a sound theory; and one that describes process, not only typologies.

Probationary periods

Probation is defined as 'The subjection of an individual to a period of testing to ascertain fitness for a job'. Etymologically, the word means to prove, to substantiate and to validate.

In most jobs, there is, or at least was, what was called a 'probationary period' ranging from a month to three years. It was 'a time of trial', where supposedly both sides – employer and employee – were able to revisit their selection decision. Had both chosen wisely? At the end of the period, the employer/selector had a number of possible choices: confirm the appointment; extend the probationary period; dismiss/reject the employee.

Or so the theory went. For most, if not all, jobs there is a Reichstag rubber stamp after the probationary period. That is, the probationary period is not what it was or should be. There are essentially two fundamental questions concerning this issue: the wisdom of the probationary period and it current decline.

Psychologists have long investigated the validity of various selection devices from the big three – application form, selection interview and references – to the expensive (Assessment Centres) and bizarre (graphology). There is a great list to choose from, apart from those above, including ability tests, biographical inventories, job knowledge tests, personality tests, as well as ratings by peers and subordinates in the previous job.

Research since the mid-fifties has tried to determine which of these techniques best predicts later carefully-evaluated and measured work output. These are difficult and expensive studies, inevitably involving many thousands of people over many years. Studies over the last 25 years have tended both to be empirically better and give more consistent findings. That is, researchers with different data banks in different countries and with different criteria have found similar things.

The answer is not surprising: the big three are pretty poor at predicting job success, especially the interview, though this does not have to be the case. They are desperately unreliable. Ability tests are better predictors than personality tests. But the best predictors are things very directly related to the job, i.e. job knowledge or work-sample test or a job try-out.

What is the best predictor of job success? Yes, the probationary period. It is almost a tautology to say that how you perform is a function of how you perform. It is not feasible to give everyone a job try out, so other criteria need to be found. Alas the most expensive, i.e. the Assessment Centre, is probably the best, precisely because so much data is gathered on each person over two to three days using so many different methods like tests, interviews and observations.

A trial period of, say, 6 months with the new recruit on probation provides the ideal opportunity to validate the selection choice. Yes – they will be on their best behaviour, but so they are in the interview. Over that period, new hires need challenge and support to give them a fair go. But they also need monitoring by supervisors, subordinates and particularly by peers, who perhaps receive the best data.

It is not too difficult to observe whether the selected individual has the ability, temperament and motivation to do the job. People find it difficult to 'role-play' the ideal employee for long periods of time. They 'leak' their real attitudes and behaviours. Managers can assess their productivity, however that is measured, and their job attitudes.

Indeed, it is even possible to set certain standards for each probationary person, which they may or may not know about. These can include criteria with respect to absenteeism, lateness and customer contact, as well as productivity.

If people fail to meet these criteria in the judgement of those making the final decision, they may have their probationary period extended to give them another go. The idea is usually that circumstances have either not been sufficiently favourable or typical, or the individuals have not been appropriately helped or monitored to show their real or typical behaviour.

The other alternative is that the employer rejects the candidate after the probationary period, having decided they are not the best/ideal/most appropriate candidate. That takes confidence and courage – and an understanding of employment legislation. And this is perhaps the main cause of the decline of the real probationary period. Managerial pusillanimity in the face of litigation.

It is much harder to get a job than to keep it. No doubt for historical reasons, as well as a shift in the zeitgeist, it has become more and more difficult to sack staff. For many a weary and wary manager, the protracted and above all expensive business of litigation is simply not worth the fight. So selectors give in, accept that their decision is sub-optimal, and live with the consequences.

But the cost of caving in may well be many times more than the cost of biting the bullet. A perfunctory number-tumbling will soon reveal this. Since the 1920s, it has been known that the best worker is at least twice as productive as the bad worker. And since the 1980s, psychologists have devised the 'rational estimate' method of estimating how much workers doing the same job vary in the value of their contribution. A rule of thumb of the difference in value between a good and average worker is 40 to 70 percent.

A good employee is considered one in the top 15% and a poor employee one in the bottom 15%. So, on £30,000 a year, the value difference between good and average is between 12 and 21, while between good and poor is twice that. Being conservative and generous, consider the costs of not rejecting an average-poor worker over a working life. It may be between a quarter and half a million pounds. Not even preposterous barrister fees amount to that much.

In selection decisions, we make our beds and lie in them. But the return-if-not-satisfied option appears to be a thing of the past. The paradox is that the probationary period used wisely in probably the best selection device there is – and possibly the most economical.

R

Research

Research, observed as somewhat cynical academia, is a bit like praying. It is an activity that is private, respectable but pointless. Ask someone what they are doing and, if they say praying, you enquire no further, being embarrassed, in awe, sympathetic. One can achieve the same effect in the ivory tower by saying one is doing research.

And many people have picked up the jargon. They say, 'I am researching the problem' which is respectable and a worthy thing to do. Not everyone is convinced. Cynics think that basic research is the process of going up dark alleys to see if they are blind. They also note the self-perpetuating nature of research, believing that the most common outcome is to have two questions where there was one before. After all, re-search is to search again. Researchers know that a successful research outcome means that less, rather than more research need to be done. No experiment is a failure: it is just as useful as an example of how not to do an experiment. If an experiment works, others think that something has clearly gone wrong.

Sceptics argue that if you research enough you will find evidence in support of your theory. It tends to make you dissatisfied with the answers you currently have. Further it can be seen as copying or plagiarising the ideas of many different people at the same time.

R & D is often 'blue sky' research. It is a 'blind date' with knowledge. It means going into the unknown; thinking the unthinkable. It can mean going into the unknown without a map. Hypothesis testing is one form of research – making really new discoveries another.

Do businesses have to do research? Some argue it's essential: cheap if you want to stay in business, expensive if you do not. Others don't mind copying the innovator. The Japanese are supposed to be masters at perfecting good ideas while the British are famous for not exploiting their inventions. Part of the problem is the culture and values of the typical R & D department – and the type of people they attract.

Consider the typical departmental culture in R & D. It is a high-risk, slow feedback existence. For some, it is rather like a form of slow-drip water torture. Managers here – ex-boffins as a rule – are ponderous and decisions are slow. They tend to be consultative and can have cash-flow problems, being neither entrepreneurial nor good accountants.

R & D specialists are not people-people. High on IQ; low on EQ. Research is a hobby, a refuge, even a hiding place. Many are big boys with expensive toys. And they are deeply committed to the science. Many are otherworldly, academic types who may yearn for the long-past quiet life in academia. Many are not interested in business at all.

At the other end of the scale is the typical marketing department with its work hard, play hard philosophy. Marketeers tend to be open, friendly, carousing extroverts who prefer to measure quantity rather than quality. They are famous for their short attention spans and their dislike of detailed paper work.

High octane marketing people are not long-term planners. They reward persistence and are very customer-sensitive. The rites and rituals of marketeers revolve around energetic games, contests and conferences. They thrive on quick, tangible feedback and love awards.

Imagine the differences between the two. R & D people call customers 'users' and find them an interfering nuisance. Marketeers want a product now and that people buy in large numbers irrespective of its fancy gadgetry.

Researchers complain that they are not understood; marketeers that they cannot sell dull products.

Things might be changing particularly at the senior level. But research can remain, in all but the pharmaceutical and high-tech computer world, a dirty word for wasted money, not a respectable activity.

References

Well over ninety percent of British companies rely on three sources of data for selecting staff: the application form, the interview and references (or letters of recommendation). References are seen to be an effective, cheap way of gathering salient information on individuals by those who know them best. They are thought to contain robust, reliable, relevant observational data that is otherwise difficult or expensive to collect.

Requests for references take forms from the most open-ended to the most detailed. Perhaps the most common method is to send to the referee a letter stating that X has applied for job Y and has nominated them as referee. Often enclosed is a fairly detailed job description and, if you are lucky, a stamped reply envelope. It is probably the laziest and most inefficient method. Referees are at liberty, in effect, to write about anything from the person's IQ to EQ, sense of humour to sense of honour. They are supposed to decode the bland H-R written job description statements and comment on the candidate's ability to fulfil them. The focus is usually on ability, not personality, and rarely about motivation.

But it is certainly all about 'select-in'. One is rarely asked about honesty, integrity, mental illness – simply because they are not part of the job description. This kind of reference is a pain for referees and there is little incentive to take them seriously except in rather dubious situations – of which more anon.

The next type of reference involves a similar letter but this time requires referees to fill in 2-3 answers to specific questions about specific 'competencies' like innovation, creativity or teamwork. Here the referee may not be asked to read a job description, but offer a pen-picture of the person under various headings. For instance: 'Is the candidate a natural team-player?' 'What is the candidate's record of innovation?' From the referees' point of view, these forms are easier to fill in, though one is rarely asked how much data one has on each issue or indeed how confident one is in the answer.

A third method involves a much more detailed 'fixed' response questionnaire. These may involve yes/no answers but traditionally are more likely to involve 3-5 point ratings using descriptions such as excellent, good, above average, etc. The form contains a sort of table/grid with the 'competencies' as rows and the ratings scales as columns. It is easy for the referee to tick the boxes. Some, wisely, allow a 'Don't know' or 'Not applicable'. Others ask one referee to give quasi-percentiles thus: 'Is the candidate in the top 5, 10, 25, 50% of sales managers you have in the organisation?' Very occasionally there are more specific questions about the darker sides of behaviour at work – average rates of absenteeism; discipline incidences; letters of complaint; number of times applications for promotion are turned down.

The fourth method is a mixture of the above three except that it is conducted by telephone after the candidate has been interviewed. The company may do both: the letters of reference before the interview but use the telephone after it, to verify their opinions and doubts. But the real reason for the telephone interview is litigation. People are likely to be much more honest on the telephone, particularly if they suspect they are being recorded. There have been court cases about references based on two things: low predictive validity and defamation liability. There is precious little evidence to suggest that references are much good and some litigious-minded people know it and object. Also, the sensitive can go to court on the flimsy basis of character defamation.

References are supposed to be useful tools in screening and selection, providing helpful information on a person's ability, motivation and job-relevant experiences. But the research on the topic suggest they contain as much irrelevant as relevant information. In the jargon, the noise-to-signal ratio is simply too bad. References are most reliable and useful when structured: that is, when referees evaluate the candidates on clear, job related behaviours and where they can indicate both how confident they are in each judgement and how much data they have to go on. And they would also probably like to know that their report is confidential and will be destroyed after the decision has been made. More importantly, they should know why they have been chosen to be a referee and how their completed form will be used.

What seriously undermines the usefulness of the whole data gathering process is that the known best practice for obtaining references is so seldom followed.

Return-on-Investment in meetings

The grey men of the bottom line are rightly keen on monetary metrics to measure performance. A simple but sobering metric is the ubiquitous Return On Investment (ROI) - a sort of interest rate for business.

The trouble with many ROI calculations is that in many parts of the business both parts of the equation are difficult to measure. Often it is return that is more difficult to calculate while investment is simple. So what is the ROI of sending a potential high-flyer on an expensive management training course? You can work out the price of the air ticket, course and hotel fees, even the opportunity cost of the individual not doing his or her real job. But how do you calculate return – is it knowledge, insight, skills, gossip and how are those put into a money metric?

In the people business where tolerance of ambiguity is a necessity – almost a virtue – people talk of doing intuitive ROIs. But the bean counters rightly get nervous of this talk. They suspect the wool is being pulled over their eyes and money is being wasted. They don't want intuition, they want numbers. They want to get figures that can be put into an equation.

So how to help the number crunchers get a handle on everyday ROI issues. Best to start with that most ubiquitous of all work activities – the meeting. How to calculate investment? It is surprisingly easy. On average people work around 100,000 minutes a year. This is calculated on a ±8 hour, 220 working day year. So if a person is paid £50,000 a year they cost 50p per minute, while those on the national average wage are about 20p per minute – and our prime minister costs about £1.50 a minute.

In theory therefore we can calculate the cost of any meeting: a cabinet meeting, the synod of the Church of England, a brainstorming or blamestorming group. Take the total number of people present, calculate their cost per minute as a function of their salaries and add together; multiply by the number of minutes. Consider an easy example. The board of Acme.com meets for an hour. The chair is on £200,000 and the nine directors (vice presidents) are on £100,000 per annum. Cost of meeting £660.00.

It seems a crude but fair way of doing things. The cost of any meeting is a function of who is there, how many are there, and how long it lasts. Makers of amazing widgets and gadgets may like to invest in a cost-of-meeting calculator that can be easily 'programmed' to tick by, once the cost per minute has been established. One could get the clock to chime once £100 or £1,000 had been spent, depending on taste. For those of a visual bent, coloured lights could indicate costs; while for those who like aural reminders, various tunes could be programmed to play after certain amounts of money had been spent.

That's the investment bit of ROI. So how about returns? What do you get for your bucks? How to determine the outcome of the meeting. This is a much tougher question. It goes to the heart of what meetings are for. Each function may have a different outcome depending on the purpose of the meeting.

Communication: Meetings are about communication right? Giving information and receiving feedback; discussing what has occurred since the last meeting; providing updates and reports. This can be done via email, letters, magazines and videos – as well as meetings. One way to calculate return is to measure what people remember, or how many notes they took.

Persuasion: Meetings are about persuasion and getting commitment – or more accurately, diffusing responsibility. You were at the meeting and voted in agreement. One measure of return is decisions made and recorded. Indeed trial by jury could be measured in the same way. How long it takes for a group to be anonymous in their judgement, or at least feel able to commit themselves to a majority judgement.

Idea Generation: Brainstorming is the process of idea generation. Despite unequivocal evidence to the effect that individuals do it more efficiently than in groups, the number of ideas generated (or perhaps more importantly the quality of ideas generated) can make a nice measurable medium.

Blamestorming: These are more fun than the above and involve finding, naming and shaming actual or potential victims. What you measure is the number of suspects' names.

Morale: Some meetings are about emotions not decisions. They are about the feelgood factor. Team spirit, esprit de corps. But how to measure that – perhaps a drop in graffiti or absenteeism.

It is indeed difficult, but not impossible, working out real ROI for meetings. If nothing else, measuring the investment in terms of money can be a sufficiently sobering experience.

Seven secrets of highly successful companies

Academics love taxonomy and categorisation. It has been said that taxonomy is the beginning of science. The Holy Grail is finding the periodic table, the most profound and simple of all categorisations, for all phenomena. Scientists from all backgrounds seek to find the most simple and fundamental groupings for everything they research from blood types to bird species. Once you have a robust and sensitive taxonomy, you can begin to try to explain the cause and the consequences of these differences.

Sometimes there are competing taxonomies and passionate supporters of each system. They look to non-believers and outsiders like madmen splitting hairs but, over time, the accumulating evidence tends to support one system or the other. And eventually we come to an agreed way of looking at the world with a useful taxonomy or parsimonious list of specific phenomena.

Your fascinating, multifaceted personality can be reduced to five numbers summarising essentially your complex history, needs, hopes, wishes. Dogs, as one sees at Crufts, are grouped into a limited number of types: gun dogs, terriers, working dogs and so on. But what about ways of getting rich?

Business academics too have tried to categorise various aspects of business life that include the fundamental ways to success. Those who have studied company success and failure have argued that there are only a very limited number of ways of making it. Conveniently for those who believe in the semi-mystical number seven, that's how many there are.

- **Product Innovation:** For every product and service there is the possibility of introducing something radically new. Microwaves, malls, minibars were all product innovations in their day. Some of these fall in popularity as quickly as they rise. Remember the Walkman? And those ubiquitous silver scooters are on their way out.

  The innovation route may take lots of R & D or quite simply a good idea. It takes understanding how people behave and what they want and creating a new product that fulfils that niche. Playboy and Polaroid were good examples and Walt Disney seems a master of the art.

- **Technological Innovation:** Coming up with a new gadget can make a company a fortune. Toy manufacturers have to be leaders in this field but so are computer boffins. The idea is to come up with technology that makes some everyday task – bar coding, packing, dressing – easier, more convenient or cheaper. The zip fastener, the ballpoint pen, the teabag, the photocopier were in their day radical technology.

  Amateur inventors are always having fun trying to make better everyday appliances. Think of the corkscrews on the market; the non-stick pans and suchlike. The idea is to find cheap-to-produce, popular products that, by having a clever bit of technology, win the market. What about the widget put in beer cans to make canned beer like barrel beer. Or the airbags in cars, which are now marketed much more for their safety than their speed. Benetton, Honda, Evergreen are big companies which have tried this route to the top.

- **Relationship Route:** Everyone knows that in business it is who, rather than what, you know. And in smoked-filled rooms (of the past), CEOs do business with each other, with politicians and potentates. Bankers, arms dealers and property developers know this approach well. The skill is smoothing the path and overcoming obstacles. It may be seen as a form of making alliances and of mergers and acquisitions, but it is far less formal than this. It is much more about establishing close working relationships with crucial people. Robert Maxwell was pretty good at this but Hammer and Khashoggi were past masters. They had the ear of foreign governments and kings. Through charm, insight, superb negotiation skills and the occasional 'sweetener', they were able to build alliances that were excellent for their companies.

  The airlines are now in the same sort of business building alliances with each other as well as with hotels, travel agencies and the like. The relationship route is not unlike the marriage route: about a third fail badly and soon; a third lose their savour; but a third go on to be really successful.

- **Exploiting Competitors:** There is nothing like complacency in successful high-market-share organisations to excite the interest of those more flexible, innovative and hungry organisations in making a killing. Successful institutions can become inflexible, rigid and bureaucratic, believing they have the secret code: they have cracked it. And they operate as they always have done which can be very insensitive to market change.

  Astute observers soon spot this. They are also very sensitive to legal loopholes, the consequences of privatisation and any regulatory changes in their own or other countries. Often they are the small guys pitted against the corporate giants. Many owners of small airlines tried this (Laker, Ryan, etc).

  They show that they could be flexible when others were not; they saw they could move fast, adapt quicker and catch the public imagination. They seek to establish compatible duopolies and do their damnest to take away their clients.

- **Turnaround Route:** Some companies have the capacity to reverse declining fortunes; to re-launch and to re-brand, turning a depressing and slow decline into a great success. It nearly always takes the efforts of a very inspiring, and driven leader. It may also take fear in a work force that sees that, unless they change, they may be out of a job.

  Hotels, banks, airlines and some manufacturers have been able to reinvent themselves and become even more successful than they were in their heyday. But they need to understand their clients, the changes in the marketplace, and have the will to re-organise. It's a bit like individual therapy: it hurts, it only works on those who are really prepared to change – but it can be almost miraculous.

- **Mobilise and manipulate market forces:** Understanding consumer psychology is difficult. People are fickle, capricious and unpredictable. Children are even more so and it really does take a lot of research to understand why some toys are a flop and others an immediate success.

  People who understand the market appeal to vanity and greed, fear and snobbery, miserliness and spendthrifts. They understand that the way a service or product is labelled and advertised can have profound effects. They need to understand the demographics and the psychographics of the market. Baby boomers and generation-X make too crude a segmentation. One needs to know the market in terms of customers' aspirations and attitudes, values and vices.

The Japanese obsession with designer labels, the insecure Western fashion victim, too-frequent-business-class-passengers are types. The clever company is not only in the business of understanding supply and demand but creating and harnessing these forces for their own benefits. They might even attempt to use those forces to destroy a potential competitor. Perfume manufacturers, clothing and accessory manufacturers and advertising agencies attempt this strategy.

- **Service breakthrough:** Those in the service business know about apostles and terrorists – the former who act as free advertisements for your product because they are so delighted and the latter because they are so angry they volunteer to try to humiliate you as much as possible.

  Hotels, banks and various transportation companies know they can win over customers simply by giving consistent and exceptional service. Singapore Airlines have cracked this for 20 years, and the Mandarin hotel chain have this as their key to success. It is not only about attractiveness and brilliantly choreographed performances, but it is about taking people to new levels of service hitherto never dreamed of.

  To be checked in over complementary tea in your bedroom that has binoculars, an umbrella and a please-take-home high-quality bathrobe is pretty unforgettable. To have errors corrected immediately by a generous business recovery operation too is quite wonderful.

  It's a challenge to 'keep-it-up' and maintain levels of service, but it can and has been done.

So there seem to be a limited number of formulae for company growth. It is about innovation, interest in modernisation and participation, reading the tealeaves of market forces and providing exceptional service. It is possible to attempt all of these strategies at the same time or sequentially but it is probably unwise to try to be all things to all men.

Stress at work

Your grandparents talked about 'having nerves' and 'suffering a mental or nervous breakdown' at work. They may even have talked about people with LMF (Low Moral Fibre). Your parents may have mentioned that a friend was 'highly strung and over-sensitive' and needed tablets and very regular visits to the doctor to keep going at work. They were an exception however. You talk about stress at work, which may require extensive therapy and sabbaticals paid for by the company. And it may also involve litigation against your employer.

It is generally believed that people are more stressed at work than in the past. But is this true? And if so (or not) why is this the case? Are we becoming more neurotic with a lower tolerance for setbacks or is unreasonable and increasing pressure put on us?

Without doubt there is a large stress industry. Lawyers, counsellors and complementary medical practitioners make a fortune out of stress cases. The laws of supply and demand mean that it is in the interest of very many people to encourage people to believe and report stress. No occupation is apparently stressless: indeed all appear to exert extreme, health-threatening stress on individuals. The quiet world of academia and the frenetic world of journalism are apparently equally stressworthy. Dentists and dustmen, pilots and policemen, broadcasters and ballet dancers all supposedly suffer equally from stress.

Over the last decade there has been a radical increase in reports of stress at work. It is almost as if one is abnormal if one does not report stress: the exceptional has become the rule. The issue is rarely out of the media and favourite tele-dons, agony-aunts and celebrities are easily available for 'rent-a-quote' on how bad things are getting. And everybody, it seems, is the winner. The supposedly stressed worker gets compensation, easier duties, time off to spend with the family. Counsellors get clients; lawyers get cases; therapists get people to lie on the couch.

But also there is always a cost. And this is borne either by the fellow workers of the stressed individual who have to work harder, or by the customers of the company. Stress means less or poorer work, which means either poorer products and services – or more workers, which means higher costs. So, if your local council workers are stressed, it is directly reflected in your rates and services. It's a bit like shop lifting: the customer picks up the tab.

What is the evidence that work is becoming more stressful? What objective, longitudinal data do we have that may be used to substantiate the claim? Good data are hard to come by, but it seems one could make a very good case that the opposite is true: work is becoming much less physically (and possibly psychologically) stressful.

Much depends on two things: first, there is the historical perspective and second, there is the job focus. If one takes a historical perspective of say 100 as opposed to 20 years, it seems there is abundant evidence that most jobs are becoming much less stressful. The working week has shortened linearly and dramatically. Statutory holidays have almost doubled. Work is safer. Working conditions are altogether much better. Health and safety and work legislation has meant that the life of most workers is quite incompatible with that of their parents. It is much more difficult for employers to abuse their staff by excessive demands, arbitrary sacking and such. The trade unions, enlightened employers and philanthropic individuals and organisations have seen to it that 'life at work' has improved immeasurably over the century. It is debatable whether this change has been linear and whether the last twenty years have seen as much change as that, say, after the war. But given the increasing amount of work-related legislation, it would be surprising if a good case could not be made for steady improvement in the protection of the worker.

The second issue is perhaps more interesting and involves that still taboo topic – social class. We hear how many women now work and the intolerable pressures put upon them to juggle home and outside endeavours. Whilst it is no doubt true that there has been a dramatic increase in middle class (A & B) women working, the opposite is true at the other end of the scale (D & E). When people think of stressful jobs, they are often middle-class professional jobs. This is no surprise: it is the articulate, demanding middle class who go to court, appear on the media and fight their corner. We hear more about the stress experienced by stockbrokers than stockhands; we hear more about stress in doctors than in doctors' receptionists.

It is probably true that the changes in the quality of working life have changed more for semi- and unskilled workers than professionals. And it does seem that changes in society at large have increased stress in certain jobs. For instance, the consumer movement has probably had a most dramatic effect on teachers, lawyers, accountants and so on. Their customers are simply 'more demanding': they know more about their consumer rights and are more confident in challenging authority. The complacent professional who off-loaded responsibility and cared little about client welfare is certainly stressed to perform.

The attitudes and behaviour of young people may have made the jobs of teachers, policemen and other authority figures more difficult and the speed of technological change has no doubt caused stress in those less willing and able to acquire more skills.

But the case of generalised increasing stress at work is far from clear. For most jobs, pay and conditions have never been better. And the latter refers to everything from job security, working hours and pension schemes, to cause for dismissal.

And yet there seems massive evidence that people say they are more stressed. Why? And does stress come from within or without? That is, are some people simply more prone to stress or is it that some jobs are more stressful? The answer, of course, is both and hence the whole theory of vocational guidance of fitting round pegs in round holes. The aim is to put the more stress-resistant (or 'hardy' in the new jargon) in the more stressful job and vice versa.

One major change over the past quarter-decade is the shift in emphasis from internal to external explanations for the cause of stress. Few doubt that there are dramatic, measurable individual differences in reactions to stress. Psychologists have long documented factors in this category. Neuroticism is now called negative affectivity but it remains the same. Those prone to anxiety, depression, phobia, hypochondria, moodiness and suchlike, are most easily stressed. Whatever job they are in, they report, and feel, stress. They are unhappy and job dissatisfied whatever the nature of their job. They have 'nerves'.

Some become stressed because they don't have the ability to do the job. They may have been over-promoted in a 'Peter Principle' sort of way. For others, the problem is that the job has changed and they have not really acquired the skills or knowledge. But as well as personality and ability differences, there is also the issue of coping patterns.

There are, quite simply, both healthy and unhealthy ways of coping with stress when it arises. And these are all pretty well known through the media exposure. Modest physical exercise, joining a support group and doing a stint of serious time management is good: increasing the stimulants and depressants (pills, booze), lethargy in general and emotional outbursts are bad. Fortunately, some of these coping strategies can be taught. Whilst personality and ability are pretty immutable, coping can be changed.

The list of external stress factors is well known, and it seems ever increasing (physical conditions, travelling time, role ambiguity, short contracts, poor appraisal etc.). And they are increasingly quite valid.

But the modern trend is to explain work stress exclusively in terms of these external factors. This denial of individual responsibility is the zeitgeist of our time. Given exactly the same job, people respond differently. Improve the job conditions, the same remains true. Some people are more stress resistant than others: they can be selected for this factor or, in part, taught it.

But we are all encouraged to look outwards, to blame others, to commit what psychologists call an attribution error. This means we explain our behaviour in terms of external conditions (the boss causes me stress) but that of others in terms of internal conditions (she is stressed because of her personality). And the pendulum has swung to the actor's rather than the observer's perspective. Reports of stress are taken at face value: it is always the employer's, government's, client's fault.

It may be time for a little old fashioned re-evaluation of the cause of the problem. For 'dear Brutus, the fault lies not in our work, but in ourselves'.

Silence is golden

Big department stores think a lot about environmental modifiers. They pump particular smells into parts of their stores; they play music and musak at carefully located sites; and the lighting, warm or cold, reflected or directed, up or down, is often expensively designed and installed for a reason.

Naturally, these environmental modifiers are not there purely for the aesthetic pleasure of customers and staff. They are there specifically to increase sales and hence profit. And the theory of the process by which this (miraculously) happens goes like this: environmental modifiers are mood state changers, certain smells (baking bread, Pears soap, Earl Grey tea, Dettol), like particular music (hymns, jazz, pop songs from our teenage years) remind us of times, people and places. Both can be surprisingly quick, effective and cheap mood changers.

One recent experimental study showed what Noel Coward called 'the power of cheap music'. The intrepid psychologists persuaded an off-license owner to make attractively piled displays of both German and French wines. But they played different music on different days – prototypic Gaelic accordion and Teutonic Oompah tunes. Yes – you guessed it. Customers bought more claret when they had the appropriate accompaniment and the same was true of the hock.

Other studies found that how long a person was prepared to be on-hold on the telephone was a function of the music played. It is quite possible that the amount of money a busker in the tube or elsewhere makes is more a function not of the quality of musicianship but simply the association people have with the music.

The stores hope that the smells, lights and sounds chosen as environmental modifiers put one in a better buying mood. The smells (e.g. new car smell) might emphasise the newness or cleanliness of the product; music may (through Christmas carols) emphasise the season of giving and recovery; other modifiers may even try to increase one's randiness.

The particular modifier chosen should reflect the clientele. Blue jeans shops play music for the generation most likely to feel excited (but comfortable) in that atmosphere. Toddlers and wrinklies clearly require rather different modifiers though they are likely to be equally repulsive to a generation-X shoppers.

Sounds and smells have quite different resonance with different people. Townies are little moved by new-mown hay, and some young people have never smelt baking at home. Some soap smells may bring back pretty awful memories of school; while any antiseptic smell may be unhappily associated with hospitals. Sounds, too, can have negative as well as positive associations. The whine of the dentist's drill is not to be recommended. Further, various tunes can have deeply unpleasant associations: hymns can be equally positive and negative depending on one's early experience of religion.

Mobile phone tunes can be absolutely infuriating – jolly, tinny warblings that are unwelcome in the extreme. They may attract attention but no more happily than a police siren or a burglar alarm.

Most people are much less aware of how their environment is modified by smells and light than they are by sound. Whilst it is true that people adapt to sounds and smells surprisingly quickly (pushing them out of consciousness), they can have a powerful impact.

Take the use and abuse of background music. Black and white films show happy munitions workers and 'factory girls' swaying happily to factory music. Some surgeons operate to music. People have even been known to walk faster (and be more polite) in public places when particular music is played.

Music can distort a sense of time: it can make one feel better; it can reduce boredom. In this sense, it appears to facilitate concentration. But music only facilitates task completion if it is tedious or monotonous. Otherwise it can have the very opposite effect.

A decade ago, a paper was published on the Mozart effect. It showed a dramatic and inexplicable finding: when playing Mozart (and only Mozart), people – usually students – seem to do better on various ability tests, particularly tests of numeracy. Various explanations were put forward: one was that the unusual use of high notes somehow stimulated particular brain areas. But nearly a dozen studies failed to replicate the effect. Indeed, some showed it had a minor detrimental effect on performance.

Extroverted students often like to study with a friend. They say it helps them. They claim they can quiz each other; clarify issues and so on. Others say that they can work better with music: they say it helps their concentration. They often choose favourite discs. Adolescents often chose the maximally worst music for study: vocal, fast, familiar. This sort of music is a perfect distractant – not an attention facilitator. Playing music during a verbal comprehension task leads to problems of divided attention. The more one needs to attend carefully to details the more the need for silence.

Unless you know what people are doing and who they are, it's best not to risk environmental music. It's true for businesses and education: silence is golden.

Three of the best

Organisational psychologists have, for nearly 80 years, tried to determine the best individual predictors of work productivity. It has been known since the 1920s that the best workers are more than twice as productive as the worst. Indeed, every manager knows that there is surprising variability in the work output of their staff.

Some struggle in when there is a train strike while others rejoice in the extra day off. Some stay late to complete an urgent task while others have a sort of 'work-to-rule' mentality. Some pick up new skills quickly and easily – while for others it is a real struggle marked by resistance and apathy. Some embrace change, but for many it is a terrifying prospect to be avoided at all costs.

So what are the strongest predictors of productivity (or satisfaction)? Education, personality, values? It's a fundamental question for all assessors, interviewers and selectors. And it has very important economic consequences for any organisation.

The paradox is that we know the answer but most ignore it. And the reason lies primarily in issues around measurement. We know what the predictors are; we can measure them cheaply, efficiently and accurately – but few do. The question is, why?

The way research is done is this: people (in large numbers) are measured in all sorts of things – intelligence, personality, beliefs, attitudes. Next their performance, over time, is measured by a range of different criteria like actual behaviours (absenteeism records, output (sales figures), as well as supervisors' reports and management assessment/appraisals). Once you have enough robust, sensitive and reliable measures of work performance, these are related (statistically) to the people measures. Whilst correlations do not imply cause, they certainly indicate important, and sometimes totally explicable, relationships. And they certainly provide vitally important information for those involved in selection.

In the 1990s, three very important reviews were published. They are called meta-analyses because they are analysis of analyses. Put simply, what this involves is collecting together many hundreds of individual studies and looking for evidence of patterns in the data. And if different meta-analyses, sometimes with as many as 100,000 people being tested, give similar results, one can be pretty confident that the results are robust. Whilst they have found some differences in different sectors (manufacturing, service) and slightly different correlates of certain outcomes (customer satisfaction, absenteeism, productivity), the results were reassuringly replicative.

And the results are – in reverse order of course – integrity, stability and intelligence. This is the crucial productivity trio. They account for about a third of the variance. In other words, one third of individual productivity can be explained by these three individual difference factors. The single best predictor of success at work is **intelligence**. Intelligent people learn faster, tend to make better decisions, adapt more easily to new circumstances. The issue with intelligence is being intelligent enough for the particular job. Just as bright, but bored, children can be very disruptive at school, so it can be that people are too bright for their jobs. Some jobs are intellectually completely untaxing – dull, monotonous, repetitive – nd in this sense one can be, what the English say pejoratively, 'too-clever-by-half'. To be too bright in many jobs (e.g. the security industry) is a distinct handicap.

However, for most management jobs, intelligence is a high bonus. Combined with energy and ambition, it is the surest predictor of promotion in any organisation that is genuinely meritocratic. Bright people are better at 'tumbling the numbers', learning new languages or anticipating the future. Their intellect gives them confidence and agility.

There is some debate in academic circles whether intelligence can be divided into distinct types that are not related to each other. Thus we may have verbal, or mathematical, or spatial intelligence. Or, if you prefer the more esoteric kinds, you may like the idea of emotional or spiritual intelligence. Those opposed to splitting, called 'lumpers', argue that the evidence shows that when people take tests that measure all these supposedly different intelligences, people tend to score very high, or average, or low on them all. Because they are all inter-correlated, they argue that there is a phenomenon called general intelligence, which can be accurately and efficiently measured by good cognitive ability tests.

If this is true, why do so few organisations used IQ tests in selection? The answer is probably three-fold. First, there are ideological objections to IQ testing. For some it smacks of 11-plus selectivity; for others they hear the voice of eugenics. Some believe the tests are not valid and pooh-pooh the extensive empirical evidence mentioned above. A second problem is litigation. If people discover they have been rejected because they are not bright enough, some will claim these tests were invalid or their personal problems (e.g. dyslexia) meant the resultant score was inaccurate and hence the decision was unfair. Others believe that tests discriminate against people of particular racial groups or gender groups and that scores are inaccurate. In an increasingly litigious environment, the selectors play safe and eschew their best opportunity to measure the most predictive of individual differences.

The third reason is that some psychometricians suggest that organisations need some 'in-house' normative data. In effect, they need to know what sort of IQ scores are predictive in the organisation. What is too low, average or above average differs between different jobs in different organisations.

This means testing current employees to get some idea of the average intelligence of successful and unsuccessful people at different levels. Try getting some street-wise but uneducated CEO or marketing director to do a test that may show them in the 'slow-dull' category. The ire of the entire top team is poured on some helpless HR person. Testing simply is not worth it.

Cognitive tests, a word preferred to IQ tests, are robust, reliable, predictive and comparatively cheap. But they are not used enough. Sometimes the reason is simply precedent, sometimes ignorance, but most often fear.

The second most predictive factor at work is **emotional stability**. Its opposite, neuroticism or negative affectivity, is a powerful negative predictor of success at work. It is very clearly a 'select out' variable.

Neurotics are prone to stress, anxiety, depression, phobia and the like. They are more often absent and have lower morale. They make difficult team workers, partly because of their unpredictable moodiness. In short, they are bad news. The emotionally stable, on the other hand, are hardier. They don't bend under pressure – they tend to be more optimistic and content.

And, like intelligence, people shun the measurement of emotional stability. The most famous and widely used personality test in the world – the MBTI – owes part of its success to the very fact that it does not measure neuroticism. So whenever you get feedback, the results are okay. No one has to be told that they are unstable, which is good for trainers, consultants and neurotics alike.

Companies don't feel comfortable measuring neuroticism for the same reasons that they do not measure IQ. It's not easy, even using the usual bland euphemisms to tell people their test results show them to be highly neurotic. Naturally, they are just the type to 'take things further' and cause a fuss.

Neuroticism is harder to measure than intelligence because tests of the latter are tests of performance (time, right-or-wrong answers) while the former are like personality tests – tests of preference. People do fake on neuroticism tests. They are loath to admit their foibles and habits. All neurotics know they are; they don't like it; can't do anything about it and may not like admitting it.

But meta-analyses have shown very convincingly that this personality factor is a powerful predictor of work-related issues across all sectors. The neurotic pilot, the neurotic policeman, the neurotic surgeon, like the neurotic waiter or hairdresser are not good news. Even in the arts, neurotics are bad news.

The third factor goes under various guises: some call it '**prudence**', others '**integrity**' and still others '**conscientiousness**'. These concepts are certainly not all the same, although they are related through the concept of morality. Various studies have shown that the thing people most want in their boss is honesty – not ambition, or empathy, or a sense of humour, but being straightforward.

Integrity is related to time-keeping, to trust-worthiness. The conscientious person struggles in and stays late. They don't loaf, goof off, have dishonest sickies or seek out unproductive, time-wasting activities. They stick to the knitting; give of their best. They tend not to dissimulate and can be trusted with information and money. They tend to be respected and trusted.

In a world of egocentric moral relativism, the person with integrity is a valuable asset. It simply is not true that business ethics have to be an oxymoron. Of course, some moral codes can make a person more full of inflexibility than integrity. But integrity means that people are likely to be honest, faithful and trustworthy.

And there are quite a lot of tests of the work ethic around. Some are pretty bland, with what psychologists call high face validity: that is, the questions do not disguise what the test is trying to measure. There are also situational tests that present typical, not-that-easy-to-solve conundrums to try and establish a person's thinking around ethical issues.

Measuring integrity can also be done by an astute use of references and 360 degree reports that measure how others have experienced the prudence, morality and integrity of the target person. They really know because they witness integrity at close hand over time – and it directly affects them.

The puzzle remains this: those who read the literature know the best predictors of work success but few measure them at selection. They often waste a good deal of effort measuring all sorts of bland competencies that predict very little. Selectors must bite the bullet: they need to find reliable ways of measuring these variables in order to do their job properly.

To see ourselves as others see us

Some people clearly have more personal insight than others. We probably all know people who genuinely believe they have a sense of humour but quite patently have not. And most of us have come across individuals who quite mistakenly believe either everyone loves them or everyone is against them.

Both consultants and trainers love the 2 x 2 grid: high/low something across the top; and similarly down the side. Thus selection is about (top) good vs. bad and (side) accept vs. reject. The 'correct' boxes are 'select the good' and 'reject the bad'. Others include the well known: 'cash-cows, dogs, stars, and question mark' classification of businesses from a grid of market growth against relative market share.

One of the games consultants/trainers often play involves just one two-by-two matrix. Across the top is written 'Things I know about myself; things I do not know about myself'. This is supposedly derived from how much you solicit feedback from others – the data set of self-understanding. Down the side is 'Things others know about me; things others do not know about me'. This is supposedly derived from self-disclosure – how much you tell others about yourself. This then leaves four boxes: they are often labelled:

Arena: the public, open area where you know and they know

Facade: the hidden area where you know, but they do not (the hidden stuff is usually felt to lead to rejection)
Blind Spot: the area where they know but you do not
Unknown: where neither you nor they have any real insight

In this 2 x 2, the size of the boxes may not be equal. Counsellors believe it's best to have a big arena and a small unknown area, though they recognise that when in the role of interviewer, it is okay to have a big facade (so-to-speak).

The two least desirable patterns are to have a comparatively big blind spot or unknown area. Those who have a big blind spot act like a bull in a china shop: they have little interest in, or knowledge of, how they come across. They can be amazingly lacking in insight. The more curious is a person with a big unknown: because they neither give nor receive feedback, they are often mystery people to others and themselves. They use no energy in self-exploration or discovery. They often seem very passive but may be quite active in tightening the shell around themselves.

In business you can often see group manifestations of these patterns. Certain groups hold views about themselves not known or shared by others. Finance chappies may think of themselves as prudent, meticulous custodians of the company's money who, by controlling costs and protecting profits, ensure the survival of the company. But others see them as risk-averse, over-cautious, obsessive plodders who prevent expansion and hold the company back.

Marketeers know they are the heart of the business. They understand the customer, know the future, control the vision – though they have constantly to fight the narrow-minded, entrenched and obstructive attitudes and behaviours of Finance, Production and Sales. However, the latter often see marketeers as air-headed, flimflam merchants claiming that they are out of touch with reality and quite unused to a day's hard graft.

The Production and Engineering chappies like to think they are the only people who do the work, i.e. come up with the tangible goods that are the business. They often believe they are misunderstood, under-valued and over-worked. Others see them as obstreperous know-alls, who are completely (internal and external) customer-unfocused. In their self-centred, low EQ world, their only interests appear to be assessing raw materials, playing with expensive toys and saying no to reasonable requests.

However, the theory goes, the more they solicit feedback from others –

like instituting an internal or external customer survey or personal 360 degree feedback – the more they would really understand about themselves. And the more honestly they describe their function, the more others would really understand them. The morale is don't complain but give some and ask for feedback.

Psychologists often make the distinction between self-perception, other-perception and meta-perception. You can be good or bad at each.

Self-perception is just that: how you see yourself. We know that anorexics genuinely see themselves as overweight despite appalling evidence to the contrary. We also know some people know their limitations but others do not. There are various ways of measuring self-perception. You can ask people to estimate their own IQ or EQ and then give them give them tests objectively. The disparity reflects poor self-perception – given, of course, that the tests are valid. Similarly, you could do the same with a personality profile or even expert judges' opinion. Self-perception comes from feedback, be it the mirror, the video-records, 360-degree appraisal or the results from school tests.

Those who seek out and seek to understand feedback of all sorts tend to have a more realistic view of themselves. They can predict how they will react under stress; they know when to call for help; they know the difference between those who are ingratiating them because of their power and position and those who genuinely like them. They are neither narcissists nor self-deprecators – they have an accurate view of themselves. A rare commodity in senior managers, perhaps.

Other perception is about social sensitivity rather than about self-monitoring. It's part of understanding others' emotions, intentions, and aspirations. Clinicians are sometimes surprisingly good at this. We often call them intuitive because, faced with the same information, some people simply see more. They seem to read the signals better. They have a better grasp of human behaviour. They have clinical insight: the skill of excellent perception of others.

People with acute other-perception pick up nuances: they can understand subtle changes in non-verbal cues; they are very aware of the corporate climate; of changes of mood. By-and-large they are good news. Being sensitive to others is nearly always an advantage – unless, of course, you can only monitor the cues and not respond to them. Being sensitive and not flexible can be very frustrating for all concerned.

The third type of perception is meta-perception: your perception of others' perception of you. Or, if you prefer, meta-meta perception: your perception of their perception of your perception of them – ad infinitum. It's the skill of reading the audience; of understanding how others will behave.

Years ago, there was an acutely embarrassing late afternoon television show called 'Mr and Mrs'. Couples had to predict how the other would respond to inane domestic questions. The idea was, the better the relationship, the better people were at the task.

There is all the difference in the world between the compulsory, orchestrated applause of the East European dictator (or party political speech giver) and the rapturous, spontaneous reaction of a worshipping audience. A good speaker can tell the difference. Actors subtly change their performance once they detect the mood of the audience. Comics – by definition do it best. It's a skill and is difficult to learn.

Those without meta-perception often misjudge others. They misinterpret the feedback that they are getting.

Testing in industry

Any managing director who wants to drive his Personnel Director around the bend just has to assert: 'I can tell if they're any good in the first 30 seconds.' In these few words, the MD is positioning his selection judgment somewhere between Papal infallibility and Divine omniscience while the HR professional struggles to discern the particular variety of bull with which he is dealing.

Selection decisions are complex. It is not simply a matter of picking the most effective person for the job. The decision has to be made within a legal framework, doing justice to the applicants, and with an eye to such matters as succession planning.

Until the early 1980s, the use of psychological tests of ability and personality in British Industry was comparatively unknown. The British were always sceptical about psychology and believed one could 'sum up' a person pretty well with a glance at a CV, the grip of the handshake, the steadiness of the eye and a few perspicacious questions at the traditional interview.

But four things happened in the early 1980s to make testing not only sexy, but almost a requirement for HR professionals who talked about best practice and level playing fields. First, sudden rises in unemployment produced such unprecedented job applicant numbers that the old system could not cope. Second, there were stories, perhaps apocryphal, quoting people like the new head of British Leyland, Michael Edwardes, who supposedly used tests (more to fire than hire people) to turn around the company.

Third, equal opportunities legislation became more prominent and its effects placed selection centre stage and, as a result, transparency and fairness became dominant requirements. These three influences created the ideal growth medium for the fourth factor: the establishment, and aggressive marketing, of test publishers, one of whom still dominates the market.

Consultants soon jumped on the band wagon and by the late 1980s testing was all the rage. Graduates on the milk round sometimes reported that they had taken the same test six times while middle-aged executives could be seen on trains reading paperbacks like 'know your own personality' and 'know your IQ' in anticipation of a terrifying testing session to determine whether they were 'let go' in the new round of restructuring.

Demand was met by supply. There was a sudden growth in test publishers and Americans found for the first time that the British were interested in using tests. Ironically, massive popular interest in tests and testing was occurring just as both personality theory and classic psychometrics were in decline in the groves of academe. But authorisation to use psychological tests was one of the grounds fought over in the establishment of Chartered Psychologist status at the time by the British Psychological Society, and this exclusivity added to the tests' mystique and appeal.

And testing was not a flash in the pan. Certainly some people remained sceptical; a number even became cynical but too many people had too much at stake. Consultants made a lot of money either testing people and writing reports or else training HR people to 'certify' them to use the tests themselves. Test creators and publishers had a field day. And HR professionals enjoyed the credibility that testing gave them.

It should be acknowledged of course that testing also made a difference. It helped in decision-making and gave users a new vocabulary to describe and analyse people. Subsequent enthusiasm for the concept of competency in fact revived interest in testing rather than quenched it.

There have been blips in the field. Some damming evaluations have been published in top research journals. Employers have been sued; others have been publicly ridiculed by their choice of test, but more frequently by the use of items in the test.

So what is the state-of-the-art twenty years on? Is there a decline in test usage because of disappointment in what testing could do? Did raised expectations lead to a major decline in interest? The answer appears to be no, and every so often a new idea comes along that helps the testing business. The latest of these is **emotional intelligence**. Despite, or perhaps, because the concept was all-things-to-all-men, it soon developed a following and it did not take long for entrepreneurs to realise its potential. Tests of all sorts with no known validity soon appeared and now they can be downloaded from the web, almost free of charge.

Perhaps the best insights into the current use of testing are to think how they are used in businesses. How, when, why and which tests are used depends extensively on the sort of business that people are in.

We recognise three common organisational types with respect to tests and testing: 'bureaucracies', 'dominated' businesses and fast-moving/ultramodern. These are not mutually exclusive categories but this characterisation seems appropriate to the way industry uses tests.

1. Bureaucracies are centralist and uniform. The Civil Service is like this but then so are many of the Utilities, large multinationals, airlines and the like. They value propriety and procedure and tend to use testing because it makes the playing field more level and manageable. They take a long time deciding *on* a test, where once they had taken a long time deciding *to* test. But once the decision has been made, they invest a great deal in training and so tend to be loyal to the test even though its results are seldom fully exploited.

2. 'Dominated' businesses are the second category and these are strictly led by one person or a small group. Many 'family' businesses fall into this category. These may have an enthusiastic advocate of testing as their leader, in which case, testing happens. More usually, the task for any key employee is that he/she gets on with the leader, irrespective of what the tests say. They emphasise the boss's judgement and the inevitability of having to make that relationship work. By definition, some are almost test addicts, the others test phobics. Often these attitudes are based not on thoughtful contemplation but on some random experience they had when first encountering a test and their reaction to it. It is essentially a lottery.

3. The third category is the new electronic industries. Fast-moving, ultramodern companies are having to move at breakneck speed. They eschew procedures that slow them down and are happy to make and re-make decisions. If people work out, fine. If they do not, fine (they can go). If tests cut out work and speed up the process, then use them. Whatever the test, if it does the job, fine. In such businesses, there is little test loyalty, just opportunistic pragmatism.

So testing is alive and well, though its market is segmented by company type. And twenty years of testing has had an effect on both tester and tested. The British use psychobabble and psychometric speak with a new confidence. 'I am an extroverted non completer-finisher'; 'I don't like my boss because he is an INTJ'; 'I am not surprised she can't get a job with that Wanted Control score' are increasingly familiar lines at parties for the chattering classes. Testing, it seems, will be with us for sometime yet and continues to hold out the hope that selection decisions can be made rapidly, fairly and rigorously.

Uncertainty avoidance

After the war, a group of American and German social scientists attempted to understand the 'Mind of the Nazis'. They interviewed many of the major perpetrators, including Goering, before he killed himself, to try to get an insight into 'how they ticked'.

The result of their effort was a book called *The Authoritarian Personality*, which looked at the personality traits and processes associated with what might euphemistically be called 'interpersonal intolerance'. One trait that they identified was called intolerance of ambiguity. It is now called uncertainty avoidance or, more colloquially, 'managing the grey'. This has been identified as an important interpersonal, corporate and cultural difference factor in business life.

All of us would like to be sure we lived in a stable, predictable, just and certain world. Randomness, chaos and capriciousness are truly terrifying and we all invest a lot of energy trying to combat these forces of darkness. But our need for clarity, certainty and decisiveness differs from individual to individual and country to country.

In Britain, we have no written constitution. In the law, we muddle along on a case-by-case basis eschewing any grand *Code Napoleon*. We positively revel in subtle meaningless differences like 'The Bishop of England' (York) versus 'The Bishop of All England' (Canterbury).

Uncertainty avoidance can be considered at the national, the organisational and the individual differences level. The British can, it appears, cope with uncertainty. We are like the Indians and the Swedes and the Danes. But research indicates that other countries are rather different in this respect. The Belgians and Japanese (no surprise there), the Greeks and the Portuguese have a stronger need to avoid uncertainty.

There are, it appears, all sorts of differences between low (us) and high uncertainty avoidance cultures. Compared to those which score highly on uncertainty avoidance, cultures with lower scores are more accepting of dissent, more tolerant of deviance, more positive to the young, less risk averse, less happy about showing emotion.

But organisations and industries can also be categorised on this dimension. Indeed it is likely that the intolerant or uncertainty avoiding seek out (and even seek to change) organisations that 'fit' with their own preferences. Again, researchers who have contrasted low and high uncertainty avoiding organisations see clear differences. The more tolerant tend to less stress, live more in the present than the future, show less emotional resistance to change and tend to have more highly achievement-motivated people. Tolerant companies tend to be smaller, with a smaller generation gap and a lower average age for higher-level jobs. The ethos is that managers should be selected on ability rather than seniority, that managers need not be experts in the field they manage and that generalists are preferable over specialists.

Organisations that do not have a problem with ambiguity and uncertainty seem to favour broad guidelines over clear requirements and instructions; they believe rules may be broken for pragmatic reasons and have no problem with conflict and competitiveness. More tolerant managers are more happy to delegate, compromise and deal with 'foreigners' or people from other ethnic groups.

But it is not all good news for low uncertainty-avoidance organisations. They tend to have higher labour turnover and the job satisfaction scores of people in them are lower. Managers report and indeed have less power. But they are much less bureaucratic.

On the individual level, this simple test can provide some insight into the degree of uncertainty-avoidance you possess.

A quiz: Check T or F representing True or False for you

	T	F
1. There is always more than one right way to do anything well.	❑	❑
2. It is always better to have a definite course of action than to be vacillating and indecisive.	❑	❑
3. The best leaders give specific clear instructions so that those under them can follow them and have nothing to worry about.	❑	❑
4. Nobody can have both feelings of love and hate towards the same person at the same time.	❑	❑
5. It is better to keep on with the present method of doing things than to risk unproven methods which might lead to chaos.	❑	❑
6. An expert who won't or can't come up with a definite answer and solution probably doesn't know too much.	❑	❑
7. A good job is one where what is to be done and how it is to be done are always clear.	❑	❑
8. A person who leads a regulated and predictable life in which few surprises or unexpected happenings arise really has a lot to be grateful for.	❑	❑
9. The sooner we all acquire similar attitudes, beliefs and values the better for everybody.	❑	❑
10. It is often more fun to tackle a complicated creative problem than to solve a simple, easily solvable one.	❑	❑
11. Often the most interesting and stimulating people are those who like being different and original.	❑	❑
12. People who insist upon a yes or no answer just don't know how complicated things really are.	❑	❑
13. Many of our most important decisions have to be based upon insufficient information.	❑	❑
14. A problem has little attraction for me if I don't think it has a solution.	❑	❑
15. I have always felt that there is a clear difference between right and wrong.	❑	❑
16. Nothing gets accomplished in this world unless you stick to some basic rules.	❑	❑

17. Vague and impressionistic pictures really have little appeal for me ❑ ❑
18. I like to fool around with new ideas, even if they turn out later to be a total waste of time ❑ ❑

To get your score give yourself a point if you checked **T** for questions 1-9, 14-17, and **F** for questions 10-13, 18

The higher your score, the more you are afraid of, and made deeply uncomfortable by, uncertainty and ambiguity. People might think of you as straightforward and predictable though not creative. There are certainly areas of work where you will thrive – health and safety, production – but others where you would be deeply uncomfortable, like advertising or R&D.

V

Voluntary severance

What is the difference between voluntary severance and early retirement? Is voluntary severance more akin to (a) divorce, (b) graduation, (c) release from prison? Should one talk about severance or separation? And how voluntary is voluntary?

There are lots of ways to terminate a job. In the old days there seemed to be three major options: one got fired, one left for better/different/more appropriate work; one retired. There is a generation who had confident expectations of retirement at 65 years for men and 60 years for women. A gold watch, a comfortable pension, perhaps even an annual get together with other retirees over a good lunch and happy memories of a life-time's contribution properly recognised and feelings of a job well-done.

But this comfortable and predictable 50s picture has undergone massive changes. In some countries, the retirement age has been abolished and you can legally go on till you drop. Forceable retirement is a manifestation of ageism. Apparently, not letting people drive till they are 18 or have sex till they are 16 is not ageism – but that is another story.

But many organisations have lowered the retirement age. You *can* go at 50 but *must* go at 55. Some base it on service. So a 48-year old with 30 years service can retire in the prime of life.

The most important issue about retirement is not when but why. Strictly speaking, it is about choice: in the ideal world it is the employee's choice. When one retires depends on many things – health the cost-benefit analysis of staying (i.e. the look of the package) money saved, and the attractiveness of other work or non-work related activities.

The concept of voluntary severance is now pretty pervasive. Organisations tend to offer voluntary severance packages (VSPs) at particular times when they are trying to reduce people on the payroll. It happens traditionally after or during a merger/acquisition; a re-engineering/downsizing exercise; a bear market for the product; a major change in top management team or philosophy. Organisations recognise that people might not like the 'new situation'; are unhappy about adaptation and change and would rather leave, possibly before they are pushed. So they offer a mixture of carrot and stick. The stick is management by new tough objectives; re-skilling; re-structuring; compulsory postings to dreary subsidiaries etc.

The carrot is the VSP. The package is designed to attract the 'fifty-somethings'. And organisations, at least managers, have a very clear idea of whom they want to go. Secret lists are drawn up of the passed-over and passed-off (POPOs); the alienated troublemakers; the over-promoted and incompetent; the union-leaders and potential whistle blowers. They are subtly targeted for a VSP.

When the VSPs are announced, there is usually a good uptake. Certainly wise companies either state or at least express an optimal or maximal number of people eligible. Make the package too attractive and too many volunteer; make it insufficiently appealing and too few go. It's a hard call to get it just right. And it really is a package that may involve lump sums, pension rights and a 'goody-bag' of things like special privileges (car-parking, office space/discounts, equipment i.e. home computers). The package needs careful thought, both in terms of what things ultimately cost, but also, equally importantly, what is really attractive to the targeted population. Letting them have their work-computer may be attractive but cheap, giving car-parking space may be illegal and incredibly expensive over time.

You probably need a psychologist and an accountant to get the VSP right if you want it to do the job it is really meant for, to try and persuade the less able, motivated and talented to go.

For far too many, the consequences of the VSP are disastrous in that the talented go and the talentless stay. The situation is sometimes so serious that those who took the (generous) package have to be rehired as consultants at twice their original rate simply to keep the show on the road. They are repositors of knowledge – technological, client-based, and political. They know how things work and make them do so.

The talented, more able, people go for a variety of reasons. First, by definition, they are amongst the most able and find it pretty easy to find good work elsewhere. They are pretty confident in their abilities and have an understanding of their market value. Second, they are not neurotically attached to the organisation, feeling vengeful dependent or afraid. They may feel the organisation owes them and stays waiting for re-payment. The Freudians talk of catharsis which is the investment of psychological energy. Invest too much and it is difficult to leave.

Talented people tend to be brighter and more stable than those less so. This means they manage their money, their work relationships and their friends better. As a consequence they have probably more money to retire on if that is what they really want to do. Or they are more attractive to potential employers. So they are more likely to leave – and often on good terms, with regret mainly from the employer.

So the costly paradox is this: those who the organisations most want to go do not – and vice versa.

Virtual teams at virtual work

More and more people have a virtual company in a virtual office. It's often a large carrier bag of papers in the spare bedroom. The company might have three virtual offices – a brother's spare-bedroom in America and the parents' loft in Australia. And they (the relatives) are directors of the company. It literally has no assets – and not many more clients.

Virtual has two meanings: first, something being in essence of effect through not formally recognised or admitted; second something that is apparent rather than real. Many virtual companies are both.

But what is virtual work? Some people work in virtual teams. A virtual team is quite unlike its opposite – a real team. To be a real team means certain criteria have to be met.

- Members must be able to influence each other's beliefs and behaviours.
- They share common goals, objectives and targets.
- They have a relatively stable group structure like social rules and roles that endure over time.
- They have clear patterns of affect – liking and disliking patterns of each other.

- They recognise themselves to be part of a team.

It is business babble folklore that teams go through quite specific developmental phases. They are called forming, storming, norming, performing and adjourning. This is all about getting to know each other.

But what about a virtual team? Virtual teams are most likely individuals that come together to solve a very particular problem. They certainly are task oriented. A sort of international task-force.

In all probability the virtual team never meets but is hooked up to the web. Depending on where they are in the world, they might not even interact 'live' but merely send and receive messages. Imagine having a team member in New Zealand, twelve hours ahead of us. They check in as we clock off unless of course one is 'temporarily odd'.

Thus you may never meet (see) or talk to members of your team. The interaction is exclusively on screen. And this can cause problems as we all know with stories of email madness. It is too easy to be brusque or unclear on the web.

So often, unlike pen pals, people who meet after a longish business-email relationship are surprised by how little they know about each other – and how their impressions were wrong.

When we do business, we know there is a 'task-oriented bit' and a 'social bit'. In our culture we celebrate after work. The Japanese do the opposite. They like to get to know you, trust you – find out about your values and life style. And then do business.

Team work does not come easily to us Anglo-Saxon individualists. That is why we have to go on courses where semi-sadistic ex-corporals make you cold, wet, frightened and miserable to teach you about real interdependence in a team. You have to learn to like, trust and feel secure with individuals by seeing them in a number of different situations.

None of this happens in virtual teams. Indeed meetings may be more like casual sex encounters than one may dare to admit. There is little affect among team members. Little feeling of camaraderie; little passion except perhaps email rage and frustration.

Virtual teams in virtual organisations are virtually automatons.

There is nothing wrong with having an electronic meeting. But to pretend that people will co-operate, and thrive in virtual teams is a virtual hope, sustained by a virtual myth.

Vocational guidance

What happened to vocational guidance? It has always been a bit of a backwater in psychology and education. Some students took it seriously and there remain a few 'consultancies' who attempt to steer gormless adolescents into jobs suiting their abilities (or lack of them) and temperament.

Some have distinguished between 'fitting the job to the person' and 'fitting the person to the job'. The first is an ergonomic or software issue, the latter the essence of guidance and selection. The old metaphors talked about round pegs in round holes, which means, of course, assessing both accurately.

Who needs vocational guidance and why? It used to be seen as a science almost exclusively for callow, somewhat talentless youths. Sceptics believed that by school leaving age you should know your strengths and weaknesses (now called developmental opportunities) or at least your likes and dislikes. An alternative, of course, is to read a non-vocational arts degree that both successfully procrastinates adulthood and vocational decisions. The Oxford PPE seems to have been devised almost exclusively for the purpose.

And holiday jobs also offer an excellent opportunity to have a taster of work. A surprising number of young people take holiday employment exclusively for the money or other opportunistic reasons but find it so intriguing that they stay on. Indeed the 'year off' also provides multiple opportunities to try out various vocations without having to go to vocational guidance counsellors.

Others thought that a Darwinian process of trial and error (read hiring and firing) would give enough feedback to make an informed decision about which track to take. After all, the cost of a false start is not high and may even look good on the CV – multiple experiences and so on.

Yet there do remain some young people who simply have no idea about either their likes or abilities or motives and seek out vocational guidance. But they now seem to be in the minority. It is just as likely to be the forty-something on 'outplacement counselling' who requires what we used to call vocational guidance. The question now is what to do in the second phase of life; not what to do when starting out.

Vocational guidance used to be mainly about assessment followed by advice. Now the adult form (Outplacement Counselling) is as much about therapy as guidance. Curiously, the work-experienced seem more naive than the young and there are various reasons for this. The former may be traumatised by sudden and unexpected redundancy. They may have specialist, untransferable skills that are out-of-date. Or they may have few skills at all. They may have very little information about the world of work outside their (recently collapsed) organisation.

The outplacement counsellor may have to take a new, critical and painful look at their skills and abilities, which makes them employable. Hierarchical tables are turned: the chooser becomes the choosee; the selector the selectee. Vocational guidance was all about explaining the market; outplacement counselling is all about becoming marketable.

It is not true that you cannot teach an old dog new tricks. It just takes longer, and needs more patience and dedication. And the old dog very sincerely needs to want to learn the new tricks – not resist having to do so. Some skills are more difficult to acquire than others: particularly aspects of mental and physical dexterity which include computer skills.

Good vocational guidance, like good outplacement counselling, needs a thorough, sensitive and accurate assessment of ability and personality. This should include verbal and numerical ability as well as a set of other specialist abilities that measure what psychologists call fluid intelligence. It may be useful also to look at knowledge or crystallised intelligence and even some of the softer skills like social skills. It is also a good idea to get a measure of emotional stability and maturity, energy and drive, coping skills and the like. This is not about work style and values, decision making and relationships at work. It is about personality and intelligence.

It is of uttermost importance that the client of guidance or counselling receive honest feedback however difficult it may be to give. It is not easy to tell someone who is neurotic, dim and inadequate the truth; they may not understand what you are saying, deny the feedback – even threaten litigation. But not to tell the truth is simply to make it worse. Many highly unsuitable people long for supposedly glamorous jobs that they do not understand and for which they are profoundly unsuited. And they need that feedback: reality therapy.

The trouble with vocational guidance specialists is that they believe young people may either acquire those things found lacking in the assessment or will find out in due course the hard way. So they may deal in humbug and flimflammery so as not to offend their delicate charges. And, in doing so, they do a disservice.

Outplacement counsellors are also often guilty of pusillanimity. They argue that to give the talentless accurate feedback is to ruin their self-esteem and confidence and ensure they never get a job. The idea is that giving people negative feedback leads to vicious cycles while giving positive feedback leads to virtuous cycles irrespective of the veridicality of that feedback. But this is simply to delay the event. It is the equivalent of doctors 'lying to their patients' for their own good.

To have a realistic appraisal of one's talents definitely helps people make better decisions. It is surprising indeed to find middle-aged people so profoundly ignorant of what they are good and bad at. Perhaps it has been a lack of good appraisal from their bosses, colleagues and subordinates that has lead to this state of affairs.

And yet the problem for the vocational guidance counsellor and the outplacement assessor is not simply doing a good overhaul on the client: it is an understanding of the job. The theory is simple: you do both a person and a job analysis and then attempt to maximise the fit.

Whilst there are techniques to do job analysis (questionnaires, checklists, critical incidence analysis, diary recording), it remains poorly done. There are certain crucial features one needs to know about a job: the information and abilities required; the mental processes involved, the nature of the work output; relationships with others at work.

Three factors make job analysis difficult. First, most 'grown up jobs' are complex and multidimensional. Think of senior IT or Marketing or Engineering posts. They require all sorts of specialist and generalist knowledge; people skills; computer and financial literacy; possibly foreign language skills. They may require innovation, delegation, negotiation and investigative skills.

Second, jobs change quickly. Technology, competition and market changes mean that job analyses really need to be up-to-date – and rarely are. Even what were thought to be stable jobs like banking, teaching and the law have undergone profound changes. In some areas, you are almost out-of-date before you have finished your course. This means that vocational counsellors really need to be on the ball in all areas of the job market. This is almost a full-time task and few are. But it also means the single most desirable traits (which may be a mixture of ability and personality) are innovativeness, flexibility and adaptability to change.

Jobs change but people also move within the organisation. In the world of selection, people talk of assessing potential; that is, choosing people who will go far. This is not selecting for a job, but selecting for a series of jobs as people move up – or indeed across – the organisation. As you are promoted, you tend to do less of the things you were trained to do but manage others doing them and have to think about the future of the job and the organisation as a whole. Some people cannot make this transition and stay (or should stay) at the level they are selected for in the first place.

Pity the vocational guidance counsellor and outplacement consultant. Done well, it's quite a difficult job requiring courage and lots of research. Done badly, it does a disservice to both client and employee.

What is creativity?

A great deal of nonsense is talked about creativity. It's not an easy topic to research and few serious scientists conduct work in the area for two simple but fundamental reasons: the first is that creativity is difficult to define; the second is that there are few good ways of measuring it. If you can't agree a definition or have good tools of measurement you aren't really off the starting blocks.

Is creativity defined by a person, a product, a process or an environment? Can a person be creative without creating anything? If so, what are the personal characteristics of creative people? Can you have creative groups, rather than individuals, where somehow the group dynamic is the key to the creative process? Can you only really define creativity by the output of creative persons or groups? That is, creativity is best measured by tangible, agreed upon, outcomes.

Or is creativity a process? Is it the way painters sketch, writers scribble, sculptors carve, that makes them creative rather than some innate ability, drive or attitude? Or is it the environment that people or organisations engender that promotes creativity? Does one need funky murals, new age music, and a spirit of non-judgmental communication to be really creative?

Most people seem happy with the concept of a creative person. Many of the creative people one can mention like Van Gogh or Mozart died young, ignored, penniless and mentally ill. Later generations thought them creative but they were not recognised as such in their life times.

But if, for the sake of argument, one believes at the very minimum there must be something inside people to make them creative, the question at least for the psychologists is this – is creativity:

1. an ability?
2. a stable trait?
3. a (mood) state?
4. a thinking style?

These distinctions are not merely academic: they are fundamental to the question of whether creativity can be learnt. Various self-appointed experts claim, 'We are all creative – we just have to be taught how to liberate our talent'. But if we replace the adjective 'creative' with 'musical' or 'mathematical', it sounds quite different.

If creativity is an ability, we would expect it, like intelligence, to be normally distributed. Most physical abilities (with each sex) are like this. High jump and long jump; linguistic ability and spatial ability are normally distributed. Some people are naturally talented and an equally small number are, alas, talentless.

You measure abilities by performance tests. They are tests with correct and incorrect answers and speed of processing may also be taken into account. It was patently obvious at school that with identical tuition, some did very well at maths and others were – shall we say 'numerically challenged'. The same is true of languages: some people just seem to have an ear. If creativity is a (cognitive) ability, it can certainly be improved, but the ability level (from very bad to very good) dictates the range of improvement.

Is creativity more a personality trait, like extroversion or neuroticism? Is it a temperamental thing, possibly related to pathology? Certainly there do seem to be high incidences of similar behaviours and backgrounds in successful writers, artists and so on. But personality is like ability: normally distributed and difficult to change partly because it is 'hard-wired' and biologically based. Some introverts can pretend to be extroverts and vice versa, but it is tiring and unnatural for them and the pretence cannot be kept up for too long.

People's personalities do not change much over time. They can be seriously affected by physical or emotional trauma and certainly can be pharmaceutically altered. Anyone who has seen a depressed friend on Prozac knows what changes can occur with some specific drugs. Many creative people use drugs to help them: but as often to induce creativity as to cope with failed creativity like writer's block.

Is creativity a state, like a mood state? Can it be induced by music, watching a film, even detecting a powerfully evocative smell? Most of us may feel subjectively more creative after a couple of glasses of Chardonnay but alas the evidence is against us. True trait creatives work better when in various specific emotional states but all the drug does is get you in the mood. In fact, from the numerous confessions of very creative writers, state-altering substances (the preference is booze) rarely if ever facilitate creativity – in fact, the precise opposite.

So what about creativity as a thinking style? This is the preferred word of our time. Why? Obviously, because style involves easy change. Just as you can change your clothes and hairstyle – even political beliefs, so we are told – you can change your thinking style to become more creative. The message you hear at creativity workshops is (a) everyone is creative and (b) we can teach you to find your creativity (inner voice, inner child – blah, blah) by using techniques that alter your approach to issues. You can be taught (easily but expensively) to alter your thinking style so your 'natural creativity' can breakthrough. And so you do a bit of brainstorming, a bit of de Bonoing or whatever, and get to feel you can become a lateral thinker.

Alas there is precious little evidence to support this breathlessly exciting approach to creativity. We know scientists tend to be convergent thinkers and artists divergent thinkers. We know both can be creative in their own ways. We also know that nearly all creatives have always been that way. It is very rare to find someone who once went on a course and suddenly became creative, though it is possible – but only if they had the ability and temperament in the first place.

Alas, it is little more than a conformity myth perpetrated by workshop junkies or salesman that people can be taught to be creative. We are not all creative any more than we are all musical or mathematically gifted. You can learn to do better but only within the constraints of your God-given, biologically based, genetically determined make-up.

Work-family interface

A lot has been written about work-life balance, demands of job and family and how the one has an important effect on the other. Certainly working mothers know the real costs of this and become past masters at time management and, out of necessity, coping with stress. Senior executives now 'talk a good game' on work-life balance but rarely manifest it in themselves.

Over 40 years ago people noticed different relationships between work and leisure. For some people, their leisure was diametrically opposed to, and completely different from, their work. But for others the two were almost identical in form and function. Others kept their two worlds neatly compartmentalised. This lead to the development of three models of the relationship between the two. Some people's preferred leisure activities were almost identical to their work activity (cooks spent all their time in the kitchen at home; mechanics tinkered with their cars all weekend; pilots flew small planes for pleasure) while others did the precise opposite (security guards became parachutists; physical education teachers became weekend couch potatoes). It seems as if the one never got enough of the activity, while the other would not only want to stop doing it, but to do its opposite.

More recently these models have been successfully applied to the work-family relationship. They are quite different ways of being.

1. Spill over

This refers to the easy transfer of attitudes, feelings and behaviours from one domain (the work place) to the other (the home). It is not difficult to see how this may work. Success at work had its financial rewards (and job satisfaction), which can buy a better quality (material) lifestyle, which can increase family satisfaction.

The idea is that people choose their work and make their home in ways that are contingent with their skills, personality and attitudes. People who are neat at home are neat at work; people who like to control at home like to control at work; people who are sick at home are sick at work. We choose change and modify both our jobs and our family in line with our preferences and predictions. In a sense we create both in terms of our needs, hopes and wants.

And, in turn, we become deeply frustrated when each or both does not fit in with our desires. When you first go home with a colleague, you may be amazed by the similarities in their work style and home style. Those with paintings at work have them at home, the untidy at work are untidy at home, and the gadget obsessed has as many in the board- as the bedroom. Their lives spill over and if they are lucky, either or both are within their control. There is no discontinuity between the two. It makes the change easy, though it can lead to inappropriate behaviour, particularly in the workplace where prescribed and proscribed behaviour is much more constrained.

2. Compensation

This represents efforts to offset dissatisfaction and frustration in one domain by seeking satisfaction in the other. It is usually achieved by decreasing commitment and involvement in the one domain while increasing it in the other. Where your treasure is; there your heart is also, often where you genuinely choose to spend more time.

Compensation leads to psychological absorption and diverted attention. We all know the workaholic who finds it better being at work than at home. For the person seeming reluctant to go home, it may be quite simply that at work they are admired and supported, given private space and time, and the company of peers. At home on the other hand, they have much less personal time, feel they need to be the supporter not the supported and miss the company of adults.

Equally the home may a warm, caring, comfortable environment, while the workplace is cold, competitive, and stressful. Often, but by no means exclusively, men compensate at work, women at home. The office is a refuge for the one, while for the other it is the kitchen. The work-life balance means having more of what you want most.

There is often a male-female argument or at least it is a generational argument. Young people want to play; young adults have family duties – older adults can find themselves at work. For the middle-aged executive, power, excitement and reward is at work, not at home, while for the young mother, the only sense of control she may exert is at work.

3. Segmentation

This refers to the separation of work and family such that experience in the two domains do not influence one another. This may be seen as a natural diversion or a futile attempt to erect an unnatural boundary.

Segmentation occurs when people are totally focused on the place/domain they are currently in. Equally, people may adopt different personas and coping styles in the different places. So people may have problem-focused strategies at work but emotional-coping strategies at home. They are different people; not necessarily opposites, just different.

Just as actors in repertory can and have to be quite different characters week after week, so segmenters are compartmentalisers. They rarely worry about balance as they see the two things as unrelated to one another.

The work life balance means balancing the demands and rewards of the two environments. Those who spill over and those who segment don't have the problems of compensators who quite frankly don't want balance; they would prefer the part they don't like to completely disappear.

Which guide to witch doctors

Consultants have been described as 'simple organisms designed to translate bullshit into air miles'. And they are on the increase everywhere. Increased numbers, increased fees, increased self-confidence.

But their services remain in demand, particularly during times of serious organisational crisis like downsizing, restructuring, mergers and acquisitions. They can give disinterested advice, guide the bewildered and frightened managers and tumble numbers on relevant data they collect.

But how to choose a consultant? The choice is most often based on reputation and price, neither of which is a sensible criterion. It is much wiser to look at process, data gathering and evidence-based conclusions.

Although they all go under the guise of 'management consultants', consultants can be radically different in the way they go about the job. They differ radically in their knowledge base: some are economists, others psychologists, some have a HR background and others are statistical whizz kids. Some are techies, others counsellors – and many sell snake oil.

A business school academic remarked recently that, when he taught different age cohorts, he noticed a very clear trend. Young managers believed the solution to all business problems lay essentially in the deployment of appropriate technology; the going-on-middle-aged thought it was all about strategy and getting that right; the (well) middle-middle-aged believed it was about the most puzzling and intractable asset: people. And they either became or chose consultants with these biases.

It is not too difficult to spot these different consultant types

1. **Crypto-academics** – These are the 'wunderkinder' of the top business schools. They have MBAs, PhDs and expect sophisticated technical and statistical literacy. Their firms are like a cross between a university science department, a think-tank, and an R&D department. They think

of themselves as researchers called in to solve problems. They promise they will be able to supply theories and data and help the client make more knowledgeable decisions.

What they do is study the process with the data available. They don't do many staff interviews or conduct focus groups. They target other boffins like themselves in organisations.

They are genuinely scholarly. They write good reports in the style of academic science journals. They don't give advice as such. Like therapists, they believe you have to make the decision yourself to gain real commitment.

2. **Economic modellers –** These are the strategic planners. Most have training in economics or at least an economic view of the world. They eagerly collect the data on marketing and manufacturing from the company and the industry in general. And they feed it all into elaborate econometric models.

   The consultants are young, statistical whizz-kids with little business experience and often pretty low emotional intelligence. But they do model the business well. And they purport to tell their clients how the business really works: pull which levers to have which effects. Their interest is planning a strategy to achieve more profit, more market share, more growth. Again, don't tell the client what to do – they expect them to understand the model.

3. **Psychiatric Diagnosticians.** In business, just as in medicine, diagnosis is harder yet more important than cure. These consultants attempt to understand the real cause of the problem in organisations. They talk of systems and believe in esoteric things like organisational climate, culture, values and structure. They have a general management rather than a scientific background and are hunting down the cause of problems that inhibit their ultimate goal, which is improved organisational output.

   Like Freudians, they try to surface deep-seated problems. They know this takes time. Also the problems are often in the deep psyche of organisations. They tend to talk to lots of people. Their data is subjective self-report. And they know the implementation of solutions, like therapy, is not simple. They certainly are thorough and tend to like to have close relationships with their client.

4. **Structural Redesigners.** They believe they know the architecture and

structure of efficient organisations. And they focus on the administrative structures and procedures to make them lean and mean, logical and systematic.

They are into the business of redesign and restructuring of well-known and proved ways of doing things. The client often knows the outcome because the consultants have a system, an approach, indeed a philosophy. This is both their attraction and their disadvantage. They are technologists from many backgrounds who bought the approach.

5. **Coach-Counsellors.** These consultants offer wisdom, support and their wise counsel. They are often grey-beards with business experience, who target the CEO. They network, mentor and enjoy the role of father confessor.

   They are generalists who believe they can help the company best by helping the CEO make better judgements. They believe they act as educator, mentor, sounding board and adviser.

So crypto academics act as researchers, economic modelers as planners, psychiatric diagnosticians as doctors; structural redesigners as designers and couch-counsellors as advisers. And they promise, in that order, different things: more informed decisions; more profitable market niches; greater effectiveness; greater efficiency; and better judgement.

Some consulting firms are so big they have different departments that do different things. Some are fairly loose associations with many associates and little internal coherence.

This variety of approaches means the problem should dictate which type of consultant to choose. An organisation may need to use different consultants for different problems and to be very clear about half a dozen things:

1. What is the 'knowledge-base' of the consultants? From what background, basic discipline do they come?
2. What is their preferred relationship with the client? What role do they like to be in: adviser, designer, diagnostician, planner, researcher?
3. How do they approach the consultancy assignment? Are they agony aunts or restructurers? Are they in the business of modelling or problem identification?
4. What is the focus of their recommendations? Do they target

administrative procedures or the needs of the CEO? Are they trying to improve leadership or come up with really innovative answers?

5. What outcome should the client expect? Effectiveness or efficiency? Understanding or planning? And how do they know if it has worked?
6. What is their preferred way of working to achieve their ends? What data do they collect?

Digestif

The world is rapidly shrinking; globalisation has created a global village. Multinationals produce, sell, export and trade all over the world. There is a new breed of manager: the multinational manger who manages across boundaries. It's a tough job: tougher perhaps than managing at home. Alas, some companies deal with their sad, bad and mad managers by exporting them. They may be sent to some quiet semi-colonial outpost where hopefully 'they can do no damage'.

But are there distinct management styles? Is it possible to be competent in one culture but incompetent in another? Or is incompetence universal?

For all intents and purposes, the business world is dominated by four sub-civilisations: the Saxon, Teutonic, Gallic and Nipponic. Partly because of the formal education and informal socialisation that every culture imposes, these sub-civilisations have rather different ways of doing business and reaching decisions and overall management. There is no doubt that national (and corporate) culture does have a powerful impact on business. Culture affects feelings and relationships, how we assign status, manage time and relate to nature. It pre- and proscribes management style. It also affects how we marshal evidence, present arguments and make decisions.

The Saxon style fosters and encourages debate and discourse. Pluralism and compromise are overriding values and there is often the belief, particularly in America, that the individual should be built up, not put down. Because individuals have different perspectives and convictions, the general approach is that these differences should be debated and openly confronted so that not only a compromise but also a synthesis can be produced – a sum greater than the parts. It is via the BBC approach of thesis → anti-thesis → synthesis that clarity comes from debate. The price of ecumenism, it is believed, is anodyne blandness. Anglo-Saxons like a good natured debate: an argument supported, of course, by facts and figures and a desirable outcome.

This is quite different from the Teutonic and Gallic traditions. First, less conflict is likely to arise because, in these traditions, groups are often more homogeneous, have been selected and socialised for being 'sound on the salient issues'. Teutons and Gauls love to debate but not with antagonists, which would be considered a hopeless waste of time or an act of condescension. There is less tension-relieving humour and back-slapping – the tone is stiff, formal, caustic.

The Japanese from the Nipponic tradition don't debate, partly through lack of experience and partly because their first rule is not to upset pre-established social relations. They show respect to authority end collectivist solidarity. Questions are for clarification and debate is a social rather than an intellectual act.

The British have a penchant for documentation; the Americans for statistics. Both believe that data (reality) unite and theory divides. The British distrust theories, '-isms' and 'ologies': these are considered to be 'sweeping generalisations'. Reports, graphs and tables are seen as necessary backup to support decisions. Anglo Saxons are empiricists: they believe in collecting data and letting it speak for itself.

The Germans like fecund theories that are deductive in both senses of the word: that the theories may be deduced from other more fundamental principles and they are fecund for practical applications. It is not that they ignore data – quite the contrary – but they like to know the philosophical or economic model or theory that drives both data collection and decision making.

The Gauls are impressed by the elegance of theories and approaches. The aesthetic nature of the argument is appreciated and the way it is presented. The use of bons mots, double entendres, alliterations and allusions to obscure cultural artifacts are celebrated, not shunned. For the Teutons it is rigour before elegance, but for the Gauls it is the other way round. Sometimes the sound of words is more important than their meaning. The Germans are thorough, the French beguiling.

The Nipponese might fear inconsistency, ambiguity and contradiction but seem able to live with it. Arguments are less categorical and it is perfectly acceptable to see things as tentative, not fully formed. Ideas and theories are very cautiously elaborated with various kinds of excuses and apologies for their incompleteness.

In decision-making groups, the Anglo-Saxons pretend everyone is equal but different; the Teutonic leaders pretend that they have nothing much to learn; the Gauls that they are all irrelevant to each other and the Nipponese that they all agree. Given a proposition, the Saxons question 'How can you document or measure this?'; the Teutons want to know 'How can this be deduced from first principles?'; the Gauls, of course, wonder 'Can this be expressed in French?'; while the Nipponese approach is to ask 'Who is the proposer's boss?'

It is therefore not difficult to imagine that managers form these very different definitions of incompetence. Indeed one culture's competence maybe another's incompetence. The competent American manager may therefore be seen as incompetent in France and vice versa. Competence then, maybe culture-specific.

It is plainly true that there are national and corporate differences, which impact basic beliefs and behaviours of people at work. For instance, the degree to which decision making is centralised vs decentralised; the extent to which risk aversion or risk taking is encouraged; whether companies institute individual or group rewards; whether organisations favour short-term goals (profit, efficiency) vs long-term goals (market share, technological development).

Transnational corporations like ICI, General Electric or American Express attempt to ensure processes and procedures are the same across countries, but they try to ensure local factors are taken into account.

Indeed, there are a number of 'converging theorists' and economic determinists who argue that economic, political and social forces lead to similar economies and societies. They also argue that ideology, or values, will cease to be important because the ideology will be the same, that differences across peoples of different cultural heritages will cease to matter.

Personality plays an important part in understanding managerial incompetence. A question of considerable interest is whether the personality-incompetence relationship is universal. There are essentially three parts to this question. First, are the distribution, variability and processes in personality universal? Second, is managerial incompetence universal, in the sense that incompetent management in one sector in one country is much the same as another? Third, is the relationship between personality and incompetence universal?

At the heart of psychology there are a number of fundamental disagreements. Perhaps the best known is the nature-nurture or heredity-environment debate. It concerns whether people-psychology is essentially a biological or a social science. It has wide-ranging ramifications and it splits the discipline down the middle.

Just as cross-cultural psychologists are eager to describe, explain, and even exaggerate cross-cultural differences in human behaviour, most personality theorists prefer to celebrate the universal nature of personality functioning. Indeed over the past twenty years, there have been a number of attempts on the part of personality test constructors, to demonstrate that tests and the function or processes that they measure, are universally valid.

Personality psychologists tend to emphasise universality of personality. Researchers have shown that their tests are psychometrically valid cross-culturally. They acknowledge that man is a bio-social animal though differ in the extent to which those two halves (the biological and the social) shapes personality functioning.

Personality theorists have been eager to demonstrate that personality, as measured by established instruments, yields similar results in different cultures.

The data suggest that: the distribution of personality (trait) scores is similar across all groups, nations and races. Although there maybe very small but significant differences (i.e. the Italians are more extroverted than the Swedes), the actual differences in scores is very small indeed. Further, and perhaps more importantly, the personality process remains invariant. That is, the mechanism by which personality effects work performance is the same across cultures.

However, it is important to acknowledge that countries do business differently and that there is a noticeable effect of corporate and national culture on productivity. Thus studies show that the productivity of, say for instance, a car assembly line in country A is twice as much as in country B. This difference is not due to machine efficiency, but is usually a function of management style, corporate culture and national culture as they effect values, performance and attitudes to work.

Corporate and National Culture

In this sense, can corporate or national cultural values encourage or discourage managerial incompetence? Can a maladaptive corporate culture transform a competent manager into incompetent one?

Culture is a core concept in many of the social sciences. One of the most complete definitions of culture was formulated by Kroeber and Kluckhohn (1952) after an exhaustive historical examination of relevant literature:

'Culture consists of patterns, explicit and implicit, of and for

behaviour acquired and transmitted by symbols, constituting of distinctive achievement of human groups, including their embodiment in artifacts; the essential core of culture consists of traditional (i.e.: historically derived and selected) ideas and especially their attached values; culture systems may, on the one hand, be considered as products of action, on the other as conditioning elements of further action' (p.181).

Others are defined as thus:

'Culture is the best way we do things around here.'
Bower, 1966, cited in Deal and Kennedy (1982)

'Culture is a system of informal rules that spells out how people are to behave most of the time.'
(Deal and Kennedy, 1982)

Schein (1990) defined culture as (a) a pattern of basic assumptions, (b) invented, discovered, or developed by a given group, (c) as it learns to cope with its problems of external adaptation and internal integration, (d) that has worked well enough to be considered valid and, therefore (e) is to be taught to new members as the (f) correct way to perceive, think and feel in relation to those problems. He noted: 'For our purposes, it is enough to specify that any definable group with a shared history can have a culture and that within an organisation there can therefore be many subcultures. If the organisation as a whole has had shared experiences, there will also be a total organisational culture. Within any given unit, the tendency for integration and consistency will be assumed to be present, but it is perfectly possible for coexisting units of a larger system to have cultures that are independent and even in conflict with each other …

'The strength and degree of internal consistency of a culture are, therefore, a function of the stability of the group, the length of time the group has existed, the intensity of the group's experiences of learning, the mechanisms by which the learning has taken place (i.e. positive reinforcement or avoidance conditioning), and the strength and clarity of the assumptions held by the founders and leaders of the group.' (p11)

There is agreement over the concept of culture. First it is difficult to define (even a pointless exercise); further it is multidimensional, with many different components at different levels. It is not particularly dynamic and ever changing (being relatively stable over short periods of time). Also, it leads to significant misunderstandings (that are expected) when cultures meet. Culture shock or moving into a different corporate culture is real, painful and debilitating. Next, it represents a group solution to certain problems which may be adaptive or maladaptive; positively or negatively related to productivity. More importantly, it takes time to establish, and therefore change, a corporate 'culture'. Equally it is in many senses intangible, but has numerous observable artifacts. Finally, it is clearly linked up to implicit beliefs and values underlying behavioural norms.

Over the years two different but important approaches have been developed to describe corporate culture. The first is categorical, the second dimensional. Both provide possible insights into the way in which corporate cultures may influence management techniques.

But the clearest way to examine the effect on culture of an organisation is to see what occurs when two cultures collide in a merger. Buono, Bowditch and Lewis (1985) examined the merger of two banks, before and after the merger, and the resultant culture. Using in-depth interviews, observations and archival data, they built up a picture of the subjective and managerial culture of the two banks. Table 1 shows the categories used, and it is extremely apparent that there are major differences between the two. The authors also conducted a climate survey before and after the merger, looking at such things as organisational commitment management and supervision practice, job security and so on. The merger led to some interesting issues, such as who and from which bank to retain, and to what extent new hybrid factors/cultures needed to be invented. The post-merger survey indicated that Bank B employees felt significantly less alienated and less negative after the merger than did former Bank A employees.

Table 1: Subjective and objective organisational cultures of Banks A and B
Source: Buono, Bowditch and Lewis.
Reproduced by permission of publisher.

	Bank A	Bank B
Subjective culture		
Managerial culture		
CEO style	Participative	Authoritarian
	Egalitarian	Elitist
	'Good guy'	'Bad guy'
	'Buddha'	'Dennis the menace'
	Externally orientated	Internally orientated
Locus of power	Bureaucratic	Personal
Management style	Anticipatory	'management by crisis'
General orientation	People orientated	Task orientated
Heroes	V.P. human resources, first woman bank officer	Prior CEO, Treasurer
Mecca	Branches	'CEO's office'
Myths	'Fat cats/lazy personnel'	'Lean and mean' 'Hell hole'
When new job duties emerge	New people are hired, Highly specialised employees	Responsibility is delegated, 'jack of all trades'
Community involvement	High	Low
Objective culture		
Employee eating facility (main office)	Plush, restaurant-like	Spartan, cafeteria-like
Branches	High quality appearance (spare no expense)	Functional appearance (avoid embellishment)
CEO's office	Isolated, view of external environment	Centralised, view of internal working environment

Needless to say, the obvious and dramatic differences between the cultures of these two banks meant that the merger was fraught with difficulty. The really interesting question, however, lies in the origin of these two cultures:

how they came to be that way in the first place and to what extent the pre- and proscribed managerial activities were healthy or not. Clearly, the idea of competence as determined by Bank A was very different from Bank B. In fact, neither culture seemed particularly 'healthy'.

Describing culture and its impact

There are essentially two different approaches to describing and understanding corporate culture. The first is categorical. Various observers have attempted to describe different corporate cultures and these have nearly all resulted in a four fold categorisation (Furnham & Gunter, 1993). The categorisation appears to be based on observational/experimental data. The second approach is dimensional and is nearly always based on extensive empirical data sets.

The categorical approach seems most popular with consultants, and the dimensional approach with academics, for obvious reasons. Further, the former is particularly concerned with corporate culture while the latter extends to national culture. Both, however, provide an interesting and important insight into why specific managers may be rendered incompetent.

(a) Categorical Approaches

Deal and Kennedy (1982) identified the following four quite different types of corporate culture.

Tough-guy macho culture: This is a world of risk-taking individualists, eager for immediate feedback. Frequently, this culture is found in construction, management consultancy, venture capital, media, publishing, sports (high-risk, quick return). High-risk, high-gain philosophies abound. Heroes are survivors who win high stakes. The chance-like nature of success in this world means many superstitions, and 'comfort blanket' rituals exist. More importantly, everyone is very short-term oriented. Managers in this culture are unlikely to learn from failures or set-backs. The culture fosters immaturity and distrust of colleagues and poor teamwork. Incompetence is common in these cultures because managers take no long-term view, are poor team builders and are often deeply narcissistic.

Work hard – play hard culture: This culture encourages people to maintain a high level of relatively low-risk activity. They are found frequently in real-estate, computer companies, automotive distributors, door-to-door sales operations. Here success comes with persistence, so this is most rewarded. These cultures are deeply client/customer centered, aimed at meeting a need and filling it. Heroes are friendly, carousing, super sales people. Rites and rituals revolve around energetic games and contests and meetings. The action-oriented culture is ideal for people who thrive on quick tangible feedback – if the manager is willing and able to provide it. But quality is sacrificed for quantity. There may also be a lack of thoughtfulness and attention to detail even among senior managers. Managers can get fooled by success because of little long-term planning. High energy enthusiasts drift into cynicism when the quick-fix existence loses its meaning. Worryingly, the culture requires great respect and cultivates young people.

Bet-your-company culture: The culture is a high-risk, slow feedback existence with less pressure but 'slow-drip water torture'. This culture is found frequently in banks, mining companies, large-system business, architectural firms, computer-design companies, actuarial insurance companies. They are often ponderous, deliberate companies where good ideas are given a proper chance to show success. Decisions are slow and consultative, but top down. Heroes can cope with long-term ambiguity, and are those who respect authority and technical competence and rely upon it. These organisations move with awesome slowness, as do the senior managers who are often deeply risk-averse. These cultures are vulnerable to short-term fluctuations and cash-flow problems. They tend to favour managers who work systems well but who have low EQ.

Process cultures: This is the classic bureaucracy – a world of little feedback, where it is difficult to concentrate on outcome, so people concentrate on process. Frequently found in national government, local government, utilities, some banks and insurance companies, heavily regulated industries. These cultures are characterised by excessive reliance on memos by people trying to cover their ass. Protectiveness and caution are natural responses to the absence of feedback. Heroes are orderly, punctual, and attentive to detail. Sport/play is important – which sport, how often, who with. It is all about networking. Special language and jargon abound, which is often impenetrable. Co-worker rituals include: tough guys score points off each other; workers/players drink together; betters mentor each other; process people discuss memos.

The organisational culture influences which people are chosen to manage by selection and promotion, and how they are implicitly and explicitly trained. To this extent, different cultures may well favour people with different pathologies. Therefore the tough-guy macho culture may select out those who are bold or mischievous. Equally the work-hard play-hard cultures may seek out excitable and colourful characters. Process cultures, on the other hand, may select and socialise the diligent and dutiful types. In this sense, corporate cultures through their implicit values endorse particular management styles that may, in extremis, lead to incompetence. What they definitely do do, however, is ensure that, over time, organisations become more homogeneous in that more and more of the same type of person is recruited, selected and socialised.

What seems self-evident, is that corporate cultures must be functional, in that they develop to solve particular problems and facilitate processes and procedures. If they do not, they become dysfunctional and inhibit, rather than facilitate, business success. This Darwinian account of corporate culture may be true, where market forces apply. However, in monopolies or duopolies and often in public sector organisations, this does not apply and one often sees organisations that select and socialise for incompetence.

(b) Dimensional Approach

From his extensive database collected throughout IBM, Hofstede (1980) developed four 'dimensions' of culture – power distance, uncertainty avoidance, individualism and masculine/feminine – against which he was then able to plot 40 different nationalities. His study showed that within one multinational organisational culture, there can be marked differences based on national norms. Using Hofstede's dimensions, various researchers have proposed to select and carry out culturally sensitive interventions in overseas organisational development.

Hofstede's dimensions are as follows:

- **Power distance(PD):** The extent to which the less powerful members of institutions and organisations accept the fact that power is distributed unequally.
- **Masculinity/femininity (MF):** The extent to which the dominant values of masculine society are success, money and things, or of feminine society, caring for others and the quality of life prevailing in the organisation.

- **Uncertainty avoidance (UA):** The extent to which people feel threatened by ambiguous situations, and have created beliefs and processes that try to avoid them.
- **Individualism/collectivism (IC):** This reflects a belief that people are supposed to look after themselves and their immediate family as opposed to a situation in which people belong to in-groups or collectives, which are supposed to look after them in exchange for loyalty.

More importantly, these national characteristics can be applied to organisations. Thus, all organisations can be described in terms of their score on the four dimensions of corporate culture.

The consequences of the four cultural difference dimensions

Consequences Derived from the Power Distance Dimension

High Power Distance Countries	Low Power Distance Countries
• Decision making highly centralised	• Decentralisation of decision making
• Large pay and status differentials	• Small pay and status differentials
• Acceptance of authority and deference to the leader	• Expectations of involvement and non-deferential subordinate-superior relations
• Control of information by organisation heads/leaders	• Open information and communication systems

Consequences Derived from the Uncertainty Avoidance Dimension

High Uncertainty Avoidance	Low Uncertainty Avoidance
• Greater organisational formality and formalisation.	• Less organisational formality and formalisation
• Extensive use of policies, rules and procedures.	• Limited use of policies, rules and procedures.
• More use made of specialists. Organisations value and strive for heterogeneity	• More use made of generalists. Organisations value and encourage heterogeneity
• Attention to detail emphasised.	• Attention to strategy and the bigger picture.

Consequences Derived from the Individualist-Collectivist Dimension

Collectivist Countries	Individualist Countries
• Tendency to view the organisation as a family and to expect to be looked after like a family member	• Organisations are viewed neutrally and there are limited expectations of the organisation in terms of the personal life of members.
• Engagement with the organisation is on a moral basis	• Engagement with the organisation is on a calculative basis.
• Employees will reciprocate with loyalty and obedience to organisations who protect their interests	• Employees will stay with the organisation only as long as the exchange relationship is relatively positive.
• Holistic evaluation of persons and their performance.	• Objective, criteria-driven evaluations.
• Internal promotions.	• Open, competitive promotions.
• Personalistic relations.	• Impersonal relations.
• Group and team emphasised.	• Individual performance and expertise emphasised.

Consequences Derived from the Masculinity-Femininity Dimension

Feminine Countries	Masculine Countries
• Acceptance of those who do not value a career – both men and women.	• High expectation that men will pursue a career and will be considered as failures if they do not.
• Wary on intra-organisational competition – preference for co-operation.	• Encouragement and acceptance of intra-organisational competition.
• Supportive and encouraging behaviour is valued.	• Aggressive and assertive behaviour is valued.
• Harmony is sought and confrontation avoided.	• Conflict and confrontation are expected.

Hofstede's ideas and data electrified students of international management. Because his dimensions are data driven, it is possible to 'calculate' a culture difference score which may be an index of misfit or culture shock. Thus, imagine a Filipino going to work in America. He or she comes from a high power-distant, high uncertainty-avoidant, high collectivistic and high masculine national culture and goes to a low power-distant, high uncertainty-avoidant, high individualistic and high masculine culture.

But can this dimensional approach help us understand management incompetence? The idea that culture directs actions at work is also central to the dimensional approach. Cultures determine how people accord status to one other; how they manage time; how much they interfere with private lives; how the written and unwritten rules are developed.

It is at extremes that people or cultures become incompetent. Consider each in turn. Countries, cultures or individuals that are very high in power-distance are concerned with control and status; more than efficiency and effectiveness. Over emphasis on titles, differences and secrecy can easily lead to poor customer service. Similarly, an organisation and culture that downplays individual differences in ability, rank or status, won't understand the nature of management. It is the job of managers to get the best out of their staff: to set goals and provide support. They need to be followed and obeyed when appropriate. Further, where all information is open and communication channels free, there is a danger of information overload. Corporate cultures that reward extremely high or low power-distant behaviours are headed towards derailment.

Uncertainty avoidance at the extremes can also lead to individual and corporate derailment. Organisations that are extremely low on tolerance for ambiguity/high on uncertainty avoidance may be far too rigid in how they behave and in the rules, procedures and processes that they set for others. A great deal of business is about uncertainty and no amount of activity can change that. Issues concerning people will never be 'black and white'. Intolerance of ambiguity/uncertainty avoidance is associated with authoritarian beliefs and behaviours that are bad for business in nearly all sectors.

However, very low uncertainty avoidance individuals or cultures may also be unhealthy. Having almost no rules and procedures can lead to anarchy. People need and like predictability, controllability and certainty. One of the tasks of management is to provide just that in the right amount. Excessive risk taking and poor planning may be associated with very low uncertainty avoidance. Clearly very low scores are as dangerous as very high scores.

The dimension labelled individualism/collectivism may seem at first glance to be unrelated to incompetence. But once again, taken to extremes both approaches may lead to incompetent management. An organisation that is too collectivistic may respond too slowly, while consensus is being established. Further, it may strongly favour 'in-group' members and appoint nepotistically rather than in terms of ability. Morale issues may become more important than task issues.

The problems associated with extreme individualism are well known and self-evident. Most people at work are neither independent nor dependent on others: they are inter-dependent in the sense that they need the skills and contribution of others to ensure that their job is well done. Individuals who avoid team-work do so to the detriment of all concerned. Their apparent selfishness or indifference to the needs of others means that they score low on co-operativeness, which is essential in most modern jobs.

The final dimension called masculinity-femininity can easily be misinterpreted. It means essentially to do things in the stereotypical male vs female way. The masculine approach of conflict, confrontation and argument may be appropriate at times but can lead to lack of trust, low morale and destabilisation. Equally the feminine approach of support, caring and sharing may lead to an inability to deal with performance problems. Thus the masculine approach may be overly harsh and the feminine approach overly indulgent.

The point is that at the extremes, corporate cultures can be dysfunctional. There are in many organisations both centrifugal and centripetal forces that shift a culture to either extremes or moderate positions. Often at times of crisis, the centrifugal forces are most powerful and lead to 'extremes' of culture which may be influential in determining an organisation's stability and profitability.

Corruption and Incompetence

Is it possible to be competent in a corrupt organisation or a corrupt country? Does endemic corruption rob people, not only of their integrity, but also their ability to succeed? Individuals, organisations and countries can all be, to some extent, corrupt if they flout legal, ethical, moral and even self-advertised guidelines.

The trouble with the concept of corruption is that one person's expediency is another's misbehaviour. 'I am expeditious; he is opportunistic; they are corrupt' the saying may go. The two issues that are most talked about in business are bribery and nepotism. Business arrogance and illegal profit taking are also widely discussed. The line between sponsoring a fact-finding mission, being given a present, taken out to lunch and accepting a bribe is a thin one. Clearly in some countries (see below) and for some jobs (procurement) the temptations are high and the custom normal.

Nepotism is the appointment of people to positions based on family relationships rather than ability. Again, this can be a fine point because it could be argued that children and other relatives have a genetic disposition to be good at certain tasks. Stories of remarkable families (Bach's, Huxley's) make this theory plausible.

Of course, there are other corrupt methods in business such as mafia-type threats for protection money. More sophisticated methods involve accountancy half truths and other methods of fiddling the books.

As noted above, there may be three sources of corruption: the country, the organisation and the person. Every year, various organisations publish a corruption index that reflects the degree to which corruption is perceived to exist among public officials and politicians. The best organisations use polls. Below are the top and bottom IS countries on the 2001 index published on the web at //www.transparency.org/cpi/2001/cpi2001.html. The list goes from least to most corrupt.

The 2001 Corruption Perceptions Index

Rank	Country	Score	Surveys used
1	Finland	9.9	7
2	Denmark	9.5	7
3	New Zealand	9.4	7
4	Iceland	9.2	6
5	Singapore	9.2	12
6	Sweden	9	8
7	Canada	8.9	8
8	Netherlands	8.8	7
9	Luxembourg	8.7	6
10	Norway	8.6	7
11	Australia	8.5	9
12	Switzerland	8.4	7
13	United Kingdom	8.3	9
14	Hong Kong	7.9	11
15	Austria	7.8	7

77	Cote D'Ivoire	2.4	3
	Nicaragua	2.4	3
79	Ecuador	2.3	6
	Pakistan	2.3	3
	Russia	2.3	10
82	Tanzania	2.2	3
83	Ukraine	2.1	6
84	Azerbaijan	2	3
	Bolivia	2	5
	Cameroon	2	3
	Kenya	2	4
88	Indonesia	1.9	12
	Uganda	1.9	3
90	Nigeria	1	4
91	Bangladesh	0.4	3

Multi-nationals who operate all around the world are familiar with the problems of corruption. Corruption is subtle and leads to massive inefficiency. Everyone gets sucked into it. It is perhaps no accident that there is a correlation between corruption and GNP: the richer the country, the less corrupt.

But within countries there is interesting evidence of corruption varying from one organisation to another for all sorts of historical, social and economic reasons, and some organisations are deeply corrupt. There is widespread nepotism, bribery, 'fiddling the books'; theft and so on. The public suspects that organisations in certain sectors are less than honest and they may well be right. Curiously, recent revelations suggests that in Europe it is public corporations that are more corrupt than private corporations, whereas in America it is the reverse.

Mars (1984) studied pilfering and cheating at work, and concluded that at least some of it represented a way of hitting out at the boss, the company, the system or the state. He labelled different types of cheats at work along two dimensions. The first of the two dimensions is *grid*. Strong grid jobs limited the workers' autonomy by closely defining the tasks to be performed and the jobholders' performance expectations. Weak grid jobs gave their occupants a high degree of autonomy, and allow them to organise their work how they wished. The second dimension was *group*. This concerns how workers were free from, or subject to, group controls. In a strong group occupation, worker are under the control of fellow workers who exert and impose their views on them, whereas weak group jobs gave the individual freedom from such pressure. Mars classified occupational groups into four categories, which he called hawks, wolves, vultures and donkeys.

- **Hawks** *(weak grid, weak group).* These were the individualistic entrepreneurs, innovative professionals and small business people. However, this category also included fairground players, taxi owner-drivers and wheeler-dealer 'Mr Fixits'. The people all possessed a high degree of autonomy from group control and job definition, and this means that they could bend the rules to suit themselves. These are not high taxpayers!
- **Wolves** *(strong grid, strong group).* Employees in these occupations operate in 'wolf packs'. They pilfered according to agreed rules and through a well defined division of labour. Like a wolf pack, they have a group hierarchical structure, with a leader who gave orders, and informal rules that control the behaviour of members through sanctions. Gangs of dockers, teams of miners, refuse collection gangs and airline crews fall into this category.
- **Vultures** *(weak grid, strong group).* Vultures operated on their own when they were stealing, but they needed the support of a group in order to do it. They work in jobs that involved a large amount of moving around, and where performance success depended, to a certain degree, on an individual's flair and ability. The effect was that rules might be relaxed. Many forms of selling jobs come into this category. Hence, travelling salesmen, waiters and driver-deliverers operate vulture fiddles. Some even boast of their behaviour.
- **Donkeys** *(strong grid, weak group).* Donkeys are people who are constrained by their jobs and isolated from other workers. Transport workers, machine-operators and supermarket cashiers were all in donkey occupations. Donkeys could be either very powerful or very powerless: they are powerless if they passively accepted the constraints placed upon them, but they could exert power by rejecting such constraints, breaking the rules and thus causing temporary disruptions.

When there is a lack of fit between a person's job and his or her cosmology (ideas, values, attitudes appropriate to them), he or she will react in various ways. This is particularly true when they detect corruption in their boss or the system as a whole. They can resign (withdrawing mentally from this personal conflict); they could experience a nervous breakdown; or they can become alienated. Such alienation often results in absenteeism, employee turnover, sabotage and stealing. Thus, fiddling represents only one of a number of possible responses by an individual to a situation of work alienation. Further, the fiddles of donkeys are not fired primarily by the desire for monetary gain. Instead, the organising and operating of the fiddles provide these workers with some degree of individuality and an element of creativity which is missing from their jobs.

There can be corrupt individual managers in a corrupt-free environment. Frequently they betray their organisation or though their corrupt, unfair or prejudicial behaviours, encourage their staff's misbehaviour.

Corporate betrayal takes two forms: whistle-blowing and theft. Whistleblowers are driven by a real or perceived injustice within the company and feel it is their duty to expose it to the world. They aim to destroy the company's reputation, accusing it of acting illegally, immorally or irresponsibly. Accusations of racism, illegal underpayment, nepotism, bribery or exploitation of employees in the developing world are potentially ruinous for a company's reputation and share price.

Archer Daniels Midland (ADM) suffered huge damage when an employee, acting as a mole for the Federal Bureau of Investigation, provided evidence that the company was fixing prices for lysine, an amino acid used in animal feed. Later, ADM successfully accused the employee of embezzlement.

Some whistleblowers seek personal attention or fame, but most prefer to hide behind a veil of anonymity. A simple and shocking act, such as exposing a product as harmful will quickly be taken up by the media, which could then rally a boycott of the product. Such exposure often gives others the courage to speak out.

Blowing the whistle on one's peers is much rarer, and is frowned upon in some professions or organisations, such as medicine or the police. The recent scandal of pathologists routinely storing body parts without relatives' consent might not have gone on for so long had someone been brave enough to expose the practice.

Theft can take many forms: stealing time (through excessive absenteeism), stealing money (through embezzlement or fiddling expenses) or stealing goods. It is difficult to get accurate figures about employee theft as most companies do not know the extent of it or are too embarrassed to reveal it. However, the American Management Association estimates that $10bn-$12bn (£6.8bn-£8.2bn) is stolen from companies every year.

Psychologists talk about theft in terms of distributive justice and equity theory. Put simply, it means that employees have a clear notion of fairness when it comes to how they are treated at work. Employees often regard stealing as a way of redressing grievances or seeking revenge when they sense that their situation has become inequitable.

One study found that when employees were told their pay had to be cut, those who were given an inadequate reason for the decision stole twice as much in 'restitution' as those who were given a clear explanation.

Other research shows that when employees feel they are being treated inequitably or without dignity, they retaliate against the company by doing things they would not normally contemplate.

There is little consensus about what constitutes company theft and what occurs. Part of the problem lies in the definition of theft. In the US, the National Council on Crime and Delinquency defined it as 'a rational crime of opportunity done as an intentional act that involves a breach of trust, resulting in a direct economic benefit to the actor against the employing organisation, within varying degrees of localised tolerance'.

Theft is often a question of perception: people are happy to talk about 'taking' things – a value neutral word – from a company, but not stealing, which has strong moral overtones. Disagreement tends to lie not in whether people took something, but whether they feel the act was legitimate.

In every organisation there are driving forces that seem to encourage theft. Equally there are – or should be – restraining or inhibiting forces that will prevent it. These forces come into effect at four different levels.

First, the **individual level** – are some people more prone to steal? If so, is it because of their personality, their morality or the pressure they are under? There is considerable scientific evidence that personality is related to crime. Criminals are more likely to be extroverts characterised by risk-taking, impulsiveness and a lack of responsibility. They also tend to be tough-minded, cold and aggressive. It is curious how some people explain away criminal or immoral actions. Some try to minimise the offence ('The company can easily afford it'); others externalise it ('The boss let/made me do it'); some normalise it ('We all do that around here'); and sometimes they simply do it for kicks.

The second level is the **work group**, which often has clear rules about stealing – the amounts of various items (such as wine or stationery) considered acceptable to steal; the conditions under which theft is acceptable (the weekend, when certain people are not there); and how to do it without being caught. These informal rules may be much stronger than any formal regulations.

The third level is **organisational**. Surprisingly, there are forces operating at the organisational level that can encourage theft. It may be part of an invisible wage structure whereby supervisors reward workers with stolen goods or time off because they have no other powers at their discretion to reward loyal staff. 'Side payments' are often quicker, cheaper and more convenient than official promotions or increasing taxable salaries.

Most organisations try to prevent theft. Some offer models of ethical leadership, believing that honesty and dishonesty start at the top. Most try to specify formal practices and codes of ethics. They know if you treat people with dignity and respect, it helps: it is more difficult to steal from a company that appears to care about you.

Some companies involve employees in formally defining theft. That is particularly effective because people usually feel more committed to decisions they helped to make. If you agree that a certain act constitutes theft, it is much harder to rationalise it away. Another effective method is to tell the whole organisation the cost of stealing and how that money might be used more effectively – for example, by raising their salaries. This encourages staff to reject any 'they can easily afford it' line and even blow the whistle on each other because they know that stealing will affect them directly.

Sometimes anonymous corporate hotlines can cut down theft, while rotating work groups will help to break up clusters of people who condone stealing. Comparatively few organisations ever consider how they might spot and reject people who are predisposed to steal when they draw up recruitment and selection policies.

Finally, there is the **cultural and national level**: does loyalty to the family override loyalty to the organisation? Does loyalty to one's country come before the corporation? Globalisation offers an interesting prism through which to view corporate betrayal. It also explains why theft and betrayal may be such a big issue in one country but regarded as relatively normal in another.

Infrastructure, the rule of law, and competency

A question frequently asked, is why do some countries with few natural resources seem to thrive, while others with many fail. The question was one frequently asked of Hong Kong. Its only natural assets were a deep harbour and fresh water, which is why the British chose it for settlement. Apart from the ability and motivation of the people, many of whom fled Communism and were natural capitalists. Three explanations are typically provided. The British gave Hong Kong the rule of law; were tough on corruption and built a good infrastructure. Corruption has been considered but the other two will be briefly outlined.

At the beginning of the last century Weber argued that the Protestant Work Ethic was insufficient to ensure success. One also needs systems for monitoring, continuity and efficiency. Indeed, Weber was perhaps the first theoretical and thoughtful advocate of what we now call bureaucracy, with its rules about span of control and chain of command. Although the term now is used almost exclusively negatively, we do know that organisations, systems and structures are absolutely necessary to efficient working.

Organisations need accounting and tracking systems, as well as internal auditing. To not have these or to have systems that are overly rigid or overly lax, inevitably leads to incompetence. Internal systems need to move with the times; to be flexible but not corruptible; and to be functional. Companies need to know why they have these systems; when to update and change them.

Problems arise when good company systems must operate within poor, or non-existent, country-wide systems. This can be seen by examining first world companies and embassies working in third-world countries, because the former cannot count on the infrastructure provided by the latter. They may have even to provide their own roads, landing strips and police to ensure things work properly.

Conclusion

This book is about managerial incompetence. This *Digestif* concerns the neglected question of the universality of incompetence and whether the forces of globalisation are or will lead or more or less managerial incompetence.

I have argued that personality and personal pathology play a large part in explaining why managers fail and derail, and occasionally 'take their companies with them'. We know that these personal factors are pretty stable over time and equally distributed in all populations. Thus, this factor is likely to be equally important in all parts of the world.

However, we also recognise that organisations have their own way of doing things, and exist in a particular socio-cultural and economic setting. However competent a manager may be, the corporate and national culture might conspire to make it impossible to be efficient and effective.

		MANAGER	
		Incompetent	Competent
CULTURE	Competent	Poor selection	Success
	Incompetent	Disaster derailment doom	Managerial frustration

The above figure is rather simplistic in that it suggests that there are incompetent corporate/national cultures. By an incompetent culture we mean one in which the internal processes and procedures are not adapted to the central purpose of the organisation. We also mean one in which the basics of a modern infrastructure are there- transportation, the rule of law, absence of corruption.

Obviously, a competent manager in a competent culture means personal and organisational success. However, a competent manager in an incompetent culture (rigid, bureaucratic, corrupt) can strive to change and improve the situation. This will definitely be met by personal stress; probably organisational resistance and success will certainly not be guaranteed. It takes senior competent managers time and courage to move maladaptive, incompetent organisations into reverse; and even then, they may not succeed.

There are a lot of incompetent managers in competent organisations. A great deal of this book has describes how and why they are selected in the first place, and when and why they derail. Obviously the incompetent manager in an incompetent organisation is a recipe for disaster.

References

American Psychiatric Association (1994) *Diagnostic and Statistical Manualss of Mental Disorders*, Washington,D.C.

Adler, N. (1991). *International Dimensions of Organisational Behaviour.* Boston: PWS-Kent publishing.

Barrick, M., Mount, M., & Judge, T. (2001). *Personality and performance at the beginning of the new millennium.* International Journal of Selection and Assessment, 9, 9-30.

Barrett, P., Petrides, K., Eysenck, S., & Eysenck, H. (1998). *The Eysenck Personality Questionnaire: an examination of the factorial similarity of P, E, N and L across 34 countries. Personality and Individual differences,* 25, 805-819.

Buono, A., Bowditch, J., & Lewis. (1986). *When cultures collide: The anatomy of a merger.* Human Relations, 38, 477-500.

Caprara, G., Barbaranelli, C., Bermudez, J., Maslach, C., & Ruch, W. (2000). *Multi-variate methods for the comparison of the factor structures in cross cultural research.* Journal of Cross-Cultural Psychology, 31, 437-469.

Dalton, M., & Wilson, M. (2000). *The relationship of the five-factor model of personality to job performance.* Journal of Cross-Cultural Psychology, 31, 250-258.

Deal, T., & Kennedy, A. (1982). *Corporate Cultures.* Reading. MA: Addison-Wesley.

Furnham, A., & Gunter, B. (1993). *Corporate Assessment.* London: Routledge.

Hofstede, G. (1980). *Cultures Consequences.* California: Sage.

Hogan, R (2000) *Personality and Effective Team Peformance*, Unpublished paper

Kroeber, A., & Kluckholim, C. (1952). *Culture: a critical view of concepts and definitions*. Peabody Museum of American Archaeology and Ethnicology, 47.1.

Mars, G. (1984). *Cheats at work: An anthropology of workplace crime*. London: Adler and Unwin.

McCall, M (1998) *High Flyers*, Cambridge, Mass., Harvard University Pres

Salgado, J. (1997). *The five factor model of personality and job performance in the European Community*. Journal of Applied Psychology, 82, 30-43.

Schein, E. (1990). *Organisational culture*. American Psychologist, 45, 109-119.